The GIANT

AND HOW HE HUMBUGGED AMERICA

Jim Murphy

Scholastic Press
New York

To Al, Bruce, and Charlie —
Giants among men
and true McScummin brothers

Library of Congress Cataloging-in-Publication Data

Murphy, Jim, 1947–
The giant and how he humbugged America. / by Jim Murphy. — 1st ed.
p. cm.
Includes bibliographical references and index.
ISBN 978-0-439-69184-0 (hardcover : alk. paper) 1. Cardiff giant — Juvenile literature.
2. Cardiff (N.Y.) — Antiquities — Juvenile literature.
3. New York (State) — Antiquities — Juvenile literature.
4. Forgery of antiquities — New York (State) — Cardiff — Juvenile literature. I. Title.
F129.C27M87 2012
974.7'65 — dc23
2011036798

10 9 8 7 6 5 4 3 2 1   12 13 14 15 16

Printed in China 38
First edition, October 2012
The display type was set in I.F.C. Los Banditos.
The text was set in Hoefler.
Book design by Becky Terhune

Special thanks to Steven Diamond, Alan Gottlieb, and Nicole Durrant from
Scholastic's Photo Resource Department for their tenacious work in tracking down the art.
And to Wayne Wright, Head Librarian, Research Library, New York State Historical Association,
Cooperstown, New York, for his thoughtful and meticulous fact checking and consultation of the manuscript and art.

CONTENTS

THE CAST OF CHARACTERS

THOSE WHO DUG UP THE GIANT
Gideon Emmons

Henry Nichols

John Parker

Smith Woodmansee

THE GIANT'S ORIGINAL OWNERS
George Hull

Henry Martin

Edward Burkhardt

William "Stub" Newell

THOSE WHO FIRST SPREAD WORD ABOUT THE GIANT
John Haynes

John Clark

Silas Forbes

PEOPLE WHO BELIEVED THAT THE GIANT WAS A PETRIFIED MAN
Billy Houghton

Eugene Cuykendall

Elizah Park

Henry Dana

Miron McDonald

E. F. Owen

Ashbil Searle

EARLY BELIEVERS THAT THE GIANT WAS AN ANCIENT STATUE
John Boynton

Wills De Hass

James Hall

THOSE WHO QUESTIONED THE GIANT'S AUTHENTICITY

James Lawrence

Fillmore Smith

O. C. Marsh

Galusha Parsons

ORIGINAL SYNDICATE THAT BOUGHT THREE-QUARTERS OWNERSHIP OF THE GIANT

William Spencer

Amos Westcott

David Hannum

Amos Gillett (not mentioned by name in this book)

Simeon Rouse (not mentioned by name in this book)

Alfred Higgins (not mentioned by name in this book)

SOME OF THE LATER OWNERS OF THE GIANT

Benjamin Son

John Rankin

Calvin O. Gott

Stephen Thorne

Gardner Cowles Jr.

THOSE WHO CREATED THE GIANT'S TWIN

P. T. Barnum

George Wood

Carl Franz Otto

THOSE WHO HELPED CREATE THE GIANT

Frederick Mohrmann

Henry Salle

OTHER PLAYERS IN THE GIANT'S STORY

Lydia Newell

Joshua V. Clark

James Andrews

Andrew White

Colonel Joseph H. Wood

Avery Fellows

Thomas B. Ellis

Henry B. Turk

George Barnard

William "Boss" Tweed

Ezra Walrath

Horace Greeley

Samuel Crocker

THOSE INVOLVED IN THE *NATIONAL GEOGRAPHIC* SCANDAL

Christopher P. Sloan

Storrs Olson

William Allen

PEOPLE INVOLVED IN OTHER ARCHAEOLOGICAL FRAUDS

Johann Beringer

David Wyrick

Charles Dawson

Sir Arthur Smith Woodward

Gerrit S. Miller

Joseph Weiner

Shinichi Fujimura

Shizuo Oda

Charles T. Keally

"On Saturday morning last the quiet little village of Cardiff . . . was thrown into an excitement without precedent, by the report that a human body had been exhumed in a petrified state, the colossal dimensions of which had never been the fortune of inhabitants of the little village to behold . . ."

Syracuse Daily Courier, October 18, 1869

I.
THE DISCOVERY

The Saturday morning of October 16, 1869, was cool and damp in Cardiff, New York, as Gideon Emmons headed up the twisting dirt road. To one side, the maple and hickory trees had turned Bear Mountain into a blazing mass of yellow, orange, and scarlet leaves. It was a spectacular autumn scene, but Emmons hardly noticed. He was nursing a throbbing headache from drinking too much whiskey the night before. At 7:30 or so, Emmons met up with his friend Henry Nichols, and the two continued walking north.

They were going to William Newell's farm to dig a well for him. Nichols often did manual labor for Newell, who was his brother-in-law. He would perform simple chores, such as building stone walls, fixing leaky roofs, or cutting and stacking cornstalks. But this sort of work was unusual for Emmons.

Emmons had lost his left arm in the Civil War four years before, so he wouldn't be very useful at digging. Newell may have thought Emmons would be good at moving rocks and small stones from the hole while Nichols did the actual digging. Or he may have wanted to be charitable, since there

A view from the cornfield of Stub Newell's farm.

wasn't much work available in a farming community for a one-armed man who drank a little too much.

Twenty minutes later, Emmons and Nichols arrived at the plain white farmhouse where Newell and his wife, Lydia, lived with their young son, William Jr.

Newell, who was also called "Stub" because he wasn't very tall, greeted them and immediately led them down a sloping hill to behind his barn. The ground there was spongy and wet, and the broad expanse that stretched out before them was more like a soggy marsh than a pleasant meadow. Fortunately, Newell pointed to a dry, raised area ten feet from the barn and told Emmons and Nichols to dig the well there. He thought they might hit a good supply of water if they went down around four feet.

While the two young men began their work, Newell went back to his house where another day laborer, John Parker, waited. Newell was impatient to get his well dug and had a carefully thought-out plan for the day. While the well was being dug, he and Parker were going to select the stones that would

eventually line the inside of the well and bring them to the site. Later in the morning, a fourth man, Smith Woodmansee, would arrive to stone the well.

Newell's plan ran into trouble from the start. The ground behind the barn was rocky and bound tight by a thick growth of clover and dead tree roots. Nichols chopped and hacked at the roots and paused often to let Emmons move rocks away from the hole. After almost three hours of backbreaking work, he had only managed to dig down two and a half feet.

Newell was dumping a third load of lining stones at the well site when a loud clank rang out. Nichols had hit something solid. After banging his shovel on it several more times, Newell decided he'd hit a large stone and went to get a pick. While Newell was gone, his two workers continued to dig and clear the area around the stone. But they discovered something startling. The blue-gray stone was shaped exactly like a foot. A very large foot!

"I declare," one of the workers said, "some old Indian has been buried here!"

Emmons or Nichols shouted for Newell to come see what they'd just uncovered. Newell hurried to find out what the commotion was about, trailed by Parker and the newly arrived Woodmansee.

The five men stood around the foot, debating what they should do next. They wanted to know if they had really discovered a body, but hesitated, worried that the rest of it might be a rotting, stinking mess. Just then a horse and wagon driven by John Haynes came rattling up the road, headed for a fair in Syracuse. Woodmansee recognized Haynes and called out, "They have found a man's foot down there!"

By the time Haynes joined the others, Nichols had begun digging again. Haynes remembered looking into the hole and muttering, "It is a foot." Haynes found himself as curious as the others and eager for action. "I took a shovel and got down into the hole," he would later recall, "and as fast as they uncovered the body toward the head, I cleared the dirt off about up to the hand on the belly."

They worked quickly and managed to uncover the entire body in a matter of minutes. The diggers scrambled from the hole and all six men stood there, gazing in astonishment. Despite its being covered by a gnarly old tree root, they could see it was indeed a human body. A very old-looking one at that. And big. In fact, at ten feet, four inches long, it was nothing if not a giant.

Even though it seemed worn and eroded in places, it was very detailed anatomically, with ribs, fingernails, toenails, muscles, and Adam's apple clearly visible. But it was the facial features that truly mesmerized the men. Eyes gently closed and mouth set in a calm, straight line, the giant looked serene. As if he was sleeping peacefully and might wake up at any moment.

Someone suggested the figure might be an ancient member of the Onondaga Indian tribe. The Onondagas had once had many settlements in the area, including a large village up along Onondaga Creek, only a few miles from where they now stood. The men had grown up hearing Onondaga stories about the Stone Giants, very tall

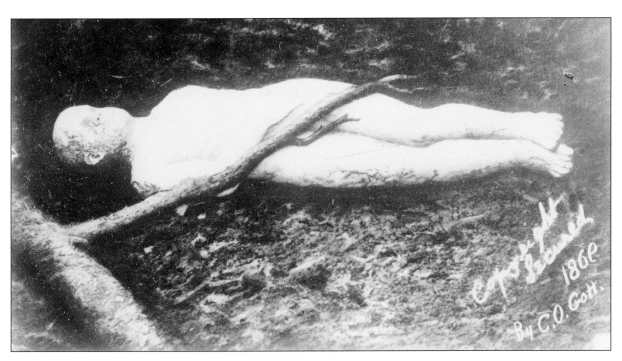

Calvin Gott took the only known photographs of the Cardiff Giant when it was still on Stub Newell's property.

creatures that terrorized the region in the distant past. They had always taken the stories to be more myth than reality. But maybe what they were staring at was proof that the giants really had existed.

Newell, though, had another, more troubling explanation. He told his friends that an earlier owner of his farm had found a long, straightedge razor in a hollowed-out tree stump. Newell said he was worried that what the previous owner had found was actually a murder weapon and that they had just unearthed the murder victim. He went on to say he did not like the thought that the killer could still be living nearby and might not like that they had found the body. Newell then proposed something almost as startling as the giant himself. He wanted to shovel the dirt back into the hole and forget about the whole thing.

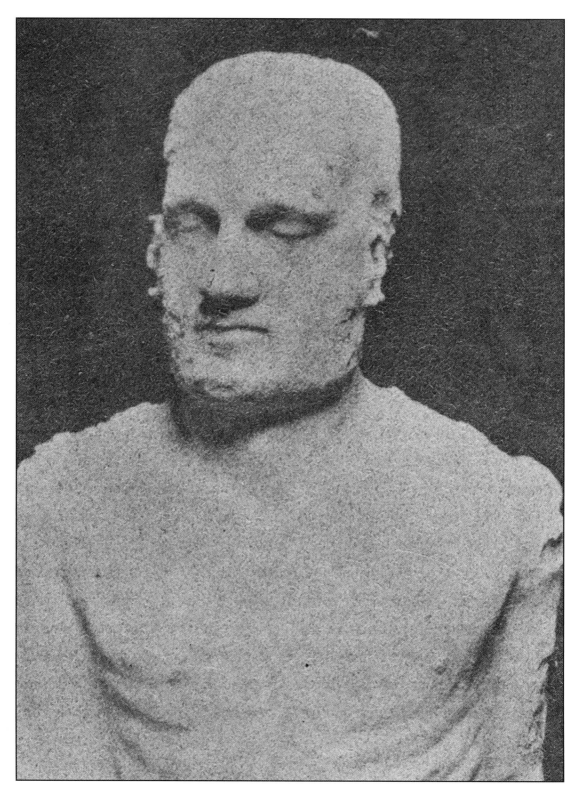

A close-up view of the Cardiff Giant.

II.
WORD SPREADS

Of course, it was already too late to hide the giant. Other folk heading toward Syracuse stopped to see why people were gathering at Newell's farm, then told others they met on the road. His hired help also spread the word when they went home. By late afternoon, a sizable and noisy crowd of men, women, and children had gathered behind Newell's barn.

There was much chatter among those assembled about what they were looking at and where it had come from. A local store owner, Billy Houghton, speculated that the giant was in fact a petrified human being, and that underground water had chemically transformed the dead man's flesh into stone. There was a buzz of agreement from the crowd. After all, hundreds of marine and plant fossils had been unearthed in area farms and quarries. Why not a human?

Oddly enough, the visitors to Newell's farm didn't seem at all surprised that there was a giant lying in the muddy hole. They had also grown up with the Onondaga stories of giants as well as legends about giants from other countries. And no less an authority than the first president of the Onondaga Historical Association, Joshua V. Clark, had reported finding numerous large fossilized skulls and bones in the town of Delphi. Clark did not realize they were the remains of mastodons and other animals, so he solemnly informed his neighbors that "the skeletons taken from [Delphi] have usually been of a size averaging far above that of common men. Several exceeded seven feet."

Another reason they didn't seem surprised was that the Bible expressly confirmed that giants had existed in the distant past. Most of the residents of Cardiff (and most of America, for that matter) had been brought up to believe that the Bible was an accurate historical record, that everything it said was literally true. There, in black and white, it told how young David had slain the giant named Goliath. And there was Og, whose very name meant "gigantic," who was killed by Moses's army at the Battle of Edrei. Very few at the Newell farm questioned the existence of giants.

As the day wore along, and more and more neighbors came to visit, ideas were offered about what to do with the giant. Many thought it might prove to be a moneymaker, and several people offered hundreds of dollars to buy it outright from Newell or to own a small share of future profits. James Andrews stunned the crowd when he offered Newell a piece of land valued at over $1,000 (which one economist estimated was equivalent to $17,000 in today's money). Andrews was a Methodist preacher, and he might have seen the giant as proof positive that the Bible was truly God's Word come true.

Newell appreciated all the offers but said he would like to sleep on them before making any decision. Others thought the giant should be removed from his grave site and brought to the fair in Syracuse. It was possible, they suggested, that someone in that sophisticated city would know something about its origins. At the very least, they added, Newell could charge money to let people take a quick glance at what everyone felt was an important discovery. Newell thought this was a good idea, and several men dashed off to get heavy ropes to haul the stone giant up.

While all this was taking place, another real concern came up. Literally.

This scene, from the biblical story told in 1 Samuel, shows young David frightening off an invading army by displaying the severed head of Goliath.

The Cardiff Giant resting in his watery grave.

Water from an underground stream was slowly filling in the hole. By the time the sun began to set, the giant was almost completely covered, and Newell fretted that the water might somehow damage his potential source of income. When the men returned with the ropes, it was completely dark and Newell decided it was now too risky to attempt to move the giant. It had lasted in the wet ground for hundreds, maybe thousands of years, he reasoned, so another night would probably not damage it much.

Lanterns were lit and Newell decided he would stand guard throughout the night. Neighbors began drifting home after this, and soon Newell was alone in the flickering yellow light, wondering what the future held for him and his giant.

III.
THE SCIENTISTS' OPINIONS

Even as Newell kept watch, word of the giant was spreading beyond the borders of Cardiff. John Clark was a lawyer and traveling temperance lecturer who had spoken in the village on Saturday evening about the evils of alcohol. Unfortunately, hardly anyone attended his talk. Afterward, he had gone to take a moonlit look at the giant, his chief rival for attention that day. Then he went back home to Syracuse. Before retiring, Clark went to a number of hotels to share news about the great find.

He soon discovered that several people had already heard about the discovery. One of the original men to see the giant, John Haynes, had traveled on to the fair and had begun spreading the news there. Another visitor to Newell's farm was Stub's nearby neighbor, Silas Forbes. Forbes had business beyond Syracuse to the north, but he went out of his way to visit the office of a local newspaper, the *Syracuse Daily Standard*, to describe what he had seen to the editor. The *Daily Standard* would call the giant "the chief topic of conversation" and estimated that over 10,000 people — one-third of the city's population — had heard about it within twenty-four hours.

Newell, of course, had no idea this

was happening. At dawn on Sunday, he finally went to bed, completely exhausted and eager for a long sleep. But it seemed that no sooner had he put his head to his soft pillow than the sounds of clomping horses and creaking wagons were heard, followed by the murmur of a gathering crowd. Most of these visitors were from surrounding villages, such as Lafayette and Tully, though a goodly number of Cardiff residents returned for a second look. By the end of the morning, visitors from Syracuse began to arrive as well.

Among the earliest visitors were people from the Onondaga tribe, who were in the city for the fair. Obviously, the Onondaga knew their ancestors had once had villages near Newell's farm and wondered if this giant was related to those from their ancient lore. Almost

An interior view of an Onondaga longhouse.

immediately, they noticed something that none of the other visitors had: The giant had distinct Caucasian features and clearly wasn't related to their past.

At about the same time as the Onondaga were making their inspection, four new visitors created a stir in the crowd. Eugene Cuykendall, Elizah Park, Henry Dana, and Miron McDonald were local doctors who asked if Newell wanted them to inspect and offer an opinion on his find. Newell accepted.

The good doctors circled the hole several times, carefully studying the prone figure and commenting to one another in whispers. It didn't seem to matter that the giant was still nearly covered with murky water, which made it hard for them to get a close or clear look at the body. After much consultation, Cuykendall, Park, Dana, and McDonald made their solemn pronouncement: The giant was indeed a petrified man.

The crowd responded to this news with an approving murmur. Here were real men of science and highly respected figures in the community who had con-firmed exactly what almost every visitor believed. A giant had lived and died right there in tiny Cardiff. The exhausted Newell perked right up when he heard this. Verification by four learned men meant his discovery was probably even more valuable than he'd originally thought.

The doctors did have a bit of negative news. They worried that the unclothed giant might provoke the village women to have sinful thoughts and suggested that it be covered. According to the *Daily Standard*, "for modesty's sake, an impro-vised 'fig leaf' was kept over the loins."

Another excited murmur rippled through the gathered crowd later in the afternoon. It turned out that the most recent arrivals from Syracuse included two newspaper reporters, an important businessman, and a celebrated lecturer on scientific matters, John Boynton.

Boynton was a notable person in the Syracuse community, though admiration for the man was tempered by what some considered his odd behavior. Boynton's career had been one of constant achievement and advancement. After attending Columbia College in New York City, and St. Louis Medical College, he set up a successful medical practice. Eventually, he turned his attention to other pursuits, including taking part in a geological survey of Lake Superior (where he discovered numerous artifacts belonging to prehistoric cultures) and as a prospector in California.

After this, he returned to Syracuse where he took up inventing, securing thirty-six patents for such items as a portable fire extinguisher, a soda fountain, a way to make carbonic acid gas (which produces the bubbles in soda), and several torpedo designs that were used during the Civil War. He added to his considerable fame and fortune by going on the lecture circuit to discuss geology, mineralogy, and relics from ancient cultures.

Despite being a very successful person, his past still trailed him. People viewed Boynton with some suspicion in large part because he had been an early member of the Church of Jesus Christ of Latter-day Saints (more commonly known as the Mormon church). This

John Boynton as he looked when a member of the Mormon church.

branch of Christianity was founded by Joseph Smith in 1830 because he believed that all other Christian churches had drifted away from the true teachings of Jesus Christ and his twelve apostles. He also said that a man could marry more than one wife and insisted that the Bible supported his position on this sensitive issue. Smith and the Latter-day Saints were criticized strongly by other religious groups and were repeatedly attacked physically.

In 1832, an angry crowd dragged Joseph Smith from a farmhouse and tarred and feathered him.

Boynton joined the Latter-day Saints two years after its founding and rose to become one of its most powerful and important leaders. And even though he later broke from the church and was excommunicated, many people still distrusted him. He made the situation worse by some of his unusual actions, which included being married in a hot-air balloon. Older, more conservative folk thought he was making fun of the sacred institution of marriage.

Boynton even managed to shock and amuse the crowd at Newell's farm.

John Boynton and his fiancée, Mary West Jenkins, moments before they sailed up in a hot-air balloon to be married.

Instead of observing the giant from a distance, the lecturer ordered that the hole be bailed of water. Then he stepped down into the oozy muck and began to dig with his fingers under the giant's neck. Once he'd done this, he cradled the head in his arms and began touching, smelling, and even licking the face for several minutes.

When the examination was finished, a mud-splattered Boynton turned to face the crowd and announced in an authoritative voice that the giant was not a petrified human. Instead, it was a man-made statue, probably sculpted by French Jesuit missionaries sometime in the seventeenth century. He went on to state that it was made of local limestone and later buried so enemies of the missionaries couldn't destroy it. Not many in the crowd agreed with Boynton, but no one openly questioned such a noted celebrity.

While everyone talked over this latest development, Boynton went to Newell and urged him to give him the giant. His reasons were simple: Only a scientist such as himself would know how to handle the giant without damaging it, and then be able to exhibit it properly. Boynton probably had other motives for wanting to control the giant. Even if it was merely an old statue, being able to display it and explain it to the public would certainly boost his reputation and his income.

Newell was still exhausted from his two long days as the giant's owner, but he was no fool. After all, he had already been offered a great deal of money for the giant; why hand it over to anyone — even a famous scientist — for free? Still, he must have said he would consider Boynton's request because the lecturer then announced that he would return the next day to fence off the giant to protect it from the curious public.

The crowd on Sunday was estimated to number well over two hundred people. With the first newspaper stories slated to appear on Monday, Cardiff and Newell would soon find themselves the hottest story in America.

IV.
OPEN FOR BUSINESS

When Newell woke on Monday morning, a crowd was already assembled on the road in front of his house. But instead of inviting everyone to step around behind the barn to see his discovery, he informed them that they would have to wait.

Newell then hired a number of neighbors to enlarge the pit and to set up a pump to drain water. Once this work was completed, he had several of them build a crude fence around the pit while the rest went to a local store to buy a tent that measured twelve by twenty-four feet. By noon, he had transformed a muddy hole into a small business and opened the flaps to visitors.

Two of his neighbors were stationed at each opening and told to collect fifty cents from anyone who wanted to view the giant. Store owner Billy Houghton (the first person to declare the stone giant a petrified man) was stationed inside the tent to tell folk about the discovery and answer their questions.

Houghton was a natural master of ceremonies. He regularly chatted up customers in his store, telling them about his line of goods, the weather, local and national politics, or whatever else might pass the time. It's possible that Newell also gave him advice, especially about playing up how ancient and mysterious the stone giant was.

One visitor, Andrew White, noticed

A small crowd outside the exhibition tent on Newell's farm.

that no matter how excited the crowd might be outside the tent, once they stepped inside the mood changed dramatically. "An air of great solemnity pervaded the place," he reported. "Visitors hardly spoke above a whisper." It was then that Houghton began his lecture.

A Syracuse newspaper took a humorous view of Houghton's show. "A man stands at the mouth of the excavation to explain the good points of the 'giant.' He . . . 'punches' the breast of the statue with a long pole, and tells you tragic words: 'He's holler there!' You involuntarily listen to see if he does 'holler,' but no sound [issues] from the finely chiseled lips, [so] you listen to the remark accompanying the next punch of the long pole. Thumping the statue near the thigh: 'He's solid there! Guess that 'ere is about the biggest leg you ever saw! Why, heavens and earth, a man could hardly reach around that leg!'"

Houghton would then go on in a dramatic voice to describe the moment the well-diggers' shovels hit the foot and how the body was uncovered. Next he might wave his pointer from the giant's toes to his head and tell how tall he was, asking the crowd to imagine such a man walking through the valley with the rest of his family. He also mentioned what the esteemed men of science had said about the discovery, though he usually shrugged aside Boynton's notion that it was a statue as "jest one feller's opinion."

Questions followed, but most people took this time to express their own ideas about the find. A few were skeptical, such as the farmer who said he would believe it was a real man only after one of the giant's legs were cut off and he could see "the marrow of his bones." Most, however, were like the woman who exclaimed, "Nothing in the world can ever make me believe that he was not a living being. Why, you can see the veins in his legs."

Some viewers noted the way the body was twisted with one arm behind the back, as if contorted in pain. Most moved beyond this sense of violence to focus on the face. "A kindly benevolent smile plays over the features," said a writer for the *New England Homestead*, "and as one looked upon it he could not help feeling that he was in the presence of a great and superior being."

Visitors on that Monday and afterward overwhelmingly believed the giant had once been a living person. They even used the word "he" when talking about the discovery. Whatever they believed, they came in droves because they needed to see the great wonder with their own eyes. Over four hundred customers went through the tent on Monday, earning Newell a neat $200 ($3,250 in today's money).

The number of visitors, which included several curious scientists, only increased in the days following as more newspaper articles began to appear. On

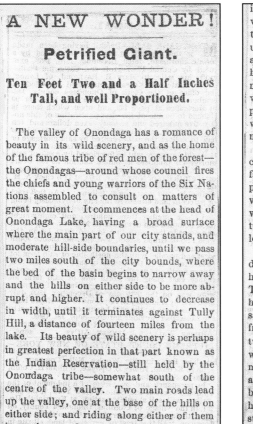

A NEW WONDER!

Petrified Giant.

Ten Feet Two and a Half Inches Tall, and well Proportioned.

The valley of Onondaga has a romance of beauty in its wild scenery, and as the home of the famous tribe of red men of the forest—the Onondagas—around whose council fires the chiefs and young warriors of the Six Nations assembled to consult on matters of great moment. It commences at the head of Onondaga Lake, having a broad surface where the main part of our city stands, and moderate hill-side boundaries, until we pass two miles south of the city bounds, where the bed of the basin begins to narrow away and the hills on either side to be more abrupt and higher. It continues to decrease in width, until it terminates against Tully Hill, a distance of fourteen miles from the lake. Its beauty of wild scenery is perhaps in greatest perfection in that part known as the Indian Reservation—still held by the Onondaga tribe—somewhat south of the centre of the valley. Two main roads lead up the valley, one at the base of the hills on either side; and riding along either of them

in a pleasant day, an admirer of nature's wild grandeur has ample occasion of admiration. The gentle slope, rising way back and up as if touching the clouds, and the more abrupt and ragged, shrub-covered, not less high hills, miniature mountains, with every now and then a ravine down which the water leaps playfully along till it reaches the plateau below and into the little creek on its way to the ocean—is a landscape of beauty not easily described.

Just now this valley is the scene of an excitement, in the finding of a supposed petrifaction of a human being—a giant. The point of interest is on the south side of the valley, opposite and just beyond the little village of Cardiff, in the town of Lafayette—twelve miles from this city, on a farm belonging to Mr. William C. Newell.

On Saturday last Mr. Newell thought to dig a well some six or seven rods east of his house, and a trifle south-east of his barn. The spot is probably thirty feet below the house, and the surface soil is a loose, half sand, half dark muck, the natural washing from the hills above. It is not more than twenty rods from the creek, the channel of which is thought to have been at or very near this spot many years ago. Mr. Newell and a hired man, in digging, had gone down but two and a-half feet when something hard was struck, which was believed to be a stone. They thought but little of it at first,

One of the first reports about the Cardiff Giant appeared in the Syracuse Daily Standard's *Monday edition.*

Monday, the *Daily Standard* ran a bold headline proclaiming: "A NEW WONDER! Petrified Giant." and explained that "just now this valley is the scene of an excitement, in the finding of a supposed petrifaction of a human being — a giant."

The *Syracuse Daily Courier* declared the giant an "IMPORTANT DISCOVERY" and said the "quiet little village of Cardiff . . . was thrown into an excitement without precedent" by a discovery that was "positively beyond the comprehension or understanding of the wise men of the valley."

By Tuesday, the giant was front-page news in New York City — with papers in Philadelphia; Baltimore; Boston; Chicago; Columbus, Ohio; Louisville, Kentucky; and as far away as San Francisco posting articles soon afterward. Telegraph messages announcing the sensational find were sent humming to hundreds of big and small towns throughout the country. The giant was also beginning to acquire a set of nicknames that included the Onondaga Giant, the Lafayette Wonder, the Petrified Giant, the Eighth Wonder of the World, the Wonder of the Age, and, of course, the Cardiff Giant.

It seemed that everyone was hungering for news about the giant, and for good reason. Between 1861 and 1865, newspapers had been filled with stories of terrible Civil War battles, along with seemingly endless lists of the 630,000 killed and over 1 million wounded. Even as the war was ending, the nation was plunged into deep mourning by the assassination of President Abraham Lincoln, which was followed by the politically turbulent years of his successor, Andrew Johnson. And just the month prior to the discovery, an attempt by Jay Gould and James Fisk to manipulate the price of gold had put the nation into a massive economic depression.

The Cardiff Giant offered readers something positive and inspiring to think about, something to distract them from more troubling news. The giant even cast his long shadow over the November elections, and one issue in particular. The United States Congress had submitted the Fifteenth Amendment to extend full voting rights to African-American citizens. Three-quarters of the states had to ratify the amendment by vote for it to become law. But even with President Ulysses S. Grant backing it, the amendment was still eight states short of passage.

The amendment had actually passed in New York in April 1869, but that didn't end the fight. Democrats opposed the measure, mainly because almost every African American who managed to vote in the previous election had done so for Republican candidates. Democrats vowed to rescind the approval if they took control of the state legislature in the upcoming election. Most Republicans also opposed the amendment, but decided to back it to gain African-American voters. The cam-

An anti–Fifteenth Amendment campaign poster with stereotypical cartoon drawing of an African American.

paign turned vicious, with name-calling and personal insults common.

But as November and the election approached, politics was no longer the main topic of conversation. The Cardiff Giant was. And newspapers (especially those backing Republican candidates) were happy to move less pleasant news to their back pages and turn their front pages over to the giant. As the *New York Commercial Advertiser* lamented, "Compared with the Cardiff graven image, the election is nowhere."

All of this attention created immense and intense interest in the giant and boosted business for Newell. Not even what is described as "extremely unpleasant, uncomfortable [wet] weather"

In addition to being one of the first to study the Cardiff Giant, Andrew White would go on to be president of Cornell University, president of the American Historical Society, and ambassador to Germany and Russia.

slowed the flow of customers. Andrew White was amazed to see "the roads . . . crowded with buggies, carriages, and even omnibuses from the city, and with lumber-wagons from the farms — all laden with passengers." On Wednesday alone, over fifteen hundred people flocked to Cardiff. Newell's first week's take was approximately $1,200 ($19,500).

The growing fame of the giant also brought Newell additional business offers. The farmer found himself increasingly involved in lengthy, secret negotiations with wealthy individuals eager to be a part of the action. There was even a rumor floating around that the famous showman P. T. Barnum was interested in purchasing the Cardiff Giant. By the end of the week, Newell had turned over the operation of the sideshow to Houghton so he could attend one meeting after another.

Just one week before, Newell was a simple and only modestly successful farmer. Now he was at the center of a story that was being talked about throughout the nation, plus he had a growing new business in place. As he prepared for bed that Friday night, he must have been very happy with the rapid turn of events in his life. What he hadn't bothered to tell any of his friends or neighbors was that his secret business negotiations were going to cause even bigger changes in the days ahead.

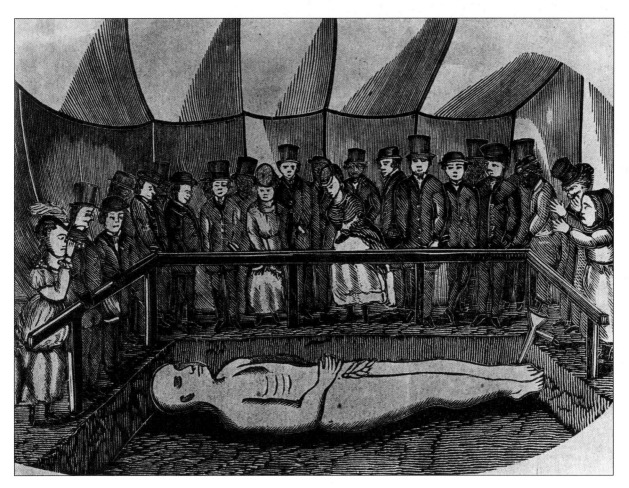

This cartoon, which appeared in a pamphlet called The Onondaga Giant, *shows the crowd inside the tent on Stub Newell's farm.*

V.
CHANGES

What had happened was very simple: Newell had decided to sell an interest in the giant to a group of men. It turned out that P. T. Barnum hadn't wanted to pursue a business deal, at least not right then. So the bidding came down to one wealthy individual and two business syndicates made up of other wealthy men.

Naturally, each time one made an offer, Newell went to the others to see if they would make a higher bid. Eventually, the two syndicates joined forces and were able to offer Newell $30,000 ($487,000) for three-quarters interest. A one-third portion of this amount was paid in cash, with the rest promised for future payment with bank notes. Newell agreed to the terms on Saturday morning with one provision — that the group allow an old friend of his, William Spencer, to also buy into the deal.

The new partners wasted little time in making changes to the existing show. The first thing they did on Saturday was hire Colonel Joseph H. Wood to run the operation. Wood was the owner of the Randolph Street Museum in Chicago and another in Philadelphia. His museums were collections of exotic stuffed animals from around the world, human oddities, and such curios as the Great Zeuglodon, a ninety-six-foot-

Albert Koch assembled this made-up sea monster in 1845 from random fossil bones and ribs and named it Hydrargos. Then he sold it to Wood, who later named it the Great Zeuglodon.

long assembly of assorted bones that Wood claimed was a prehistoric whale. Wood immediately set out to bring Newell's humble country show up to big-city standards.

Despite a downpour, he had a new and sturdier fence installed and replaced the old tent with a much larger one that could hold more people. A huge flag was hung at the head of the tent to add color and grandeur to the space, but many people objected because it was a British flag. It was soon replaced by an even bigger American flag. Making things bigger and splashier seemed to be Wood's style.

By Sunday, October 24, a wild, carnival atmosphere had taken hold at Newell's farm. "Sunday was a crusher," the *Daily Standard* reported. "The people began to go early, and kept going all day long. . . . Around the house and barns acres were covered with teams and wagons, and the road, for a long distance in either direction, was lined with them. It seemed as if such another jam never went to a show before, and it was with great difficulty that the line could be kept so that all could have a fair sight."

Another change was that a strict fifteen-minute viewing time limit was introduced to ensure a steady flow of customers. To wrangle Sunday's massive crowd of 2,300 people, Newell and his partners hired guards who, in the words of a *Daily Courier* reporter, "were compelled to bring all their powers of persuasion to effect their object." They also hired a teenager to watch over their giant moneymaker at night.

The new owners rushed into print a thirty-two-page pamphlet to provide the definitive account of the Cardiff Giant . . . at fifteen cents a copy. Whoever wrote *The American Goliah: A Wonderful Geological Discovery* seems to have taken a cue from Billy Houghton's melodramatic tent presentation. The words drip with emotion and importance: "The spectator gazes upon the grand old sleeper with feelings of admiration and awe. 'Nothing like it has ever been seen,' say all who have gazed upon it. 'It is a great event in our lives to behold it,' (is the universal verdict) —

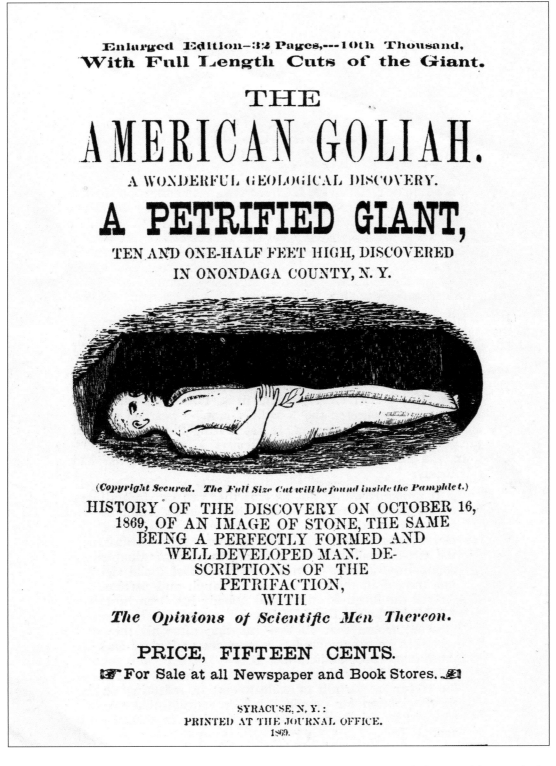

The Cardiff Giant as it appeared on the cover of The American Goliah *pamphlet. "Goliah" is a misprinting of the biblical giant's real name of "Goliath."*

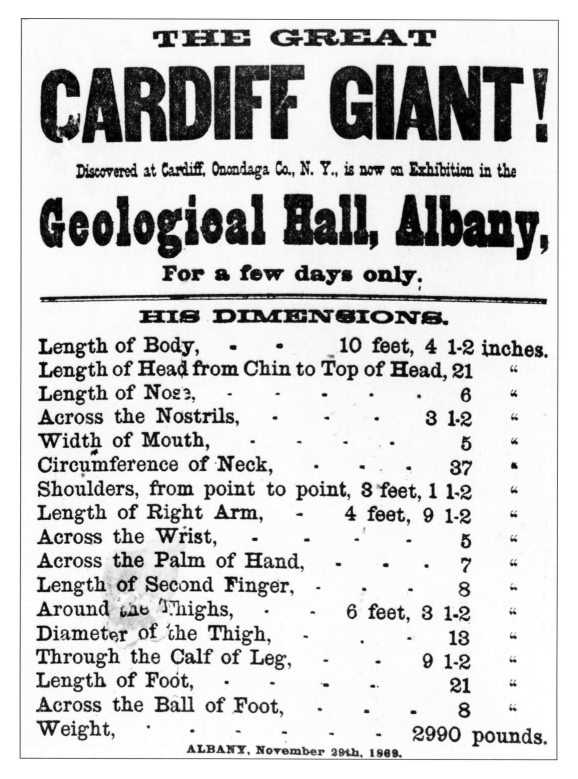

A poster for the Cardiff Giant's stay in Albany, showing his vital statistics.

'worth coming hundreds of miles for this alone.'" To help potential customers travel those hundreds of miles, the pamphlet provided specific railroad information and advice on hiring a carriage.

After describing the discovery, what the giant looked like, and listing its important dimensions, such as "Length of second finger from knuckle joint, eight inches," the pamphlet gets down to the important issue: Is the giant a petrified human being or a statue?

Using extracts from newspapers, *The American Goliah* presented evidence that the giant was a statue (quoting Boynton at length) and a petrifaction (quoting a variety of scientists and citizens at even greater length). The pamphlet clearly leaned toward the petrifaction theory. Still, the owners must have sensed that the debate itself could actually increase business since its discussion ended with: "The unsettled point of what it is, undoubtedly furnishes an additional attraction regarding the mysterious stranger, as every person wishes to see

for himself and become judge in the trial of Statue versus Fossil."

Not only did the ten-thousand-copy first edition of *The American Goliah* sell out in the first few weeks, but the crowds continued to pour in to little Cardiff. To make extra money, Lydia Newell sold gingerbread cookies and sweet cider to those waiting on the viewing line. Down the road a bit, a neighbor wanted to feed both horses and humans and hung out a sign that advertised "Warm meals, Oysters and Oats."

Already, villagers were building two taverns within five hundred feet of the Newell farm to quench the thirsts of visitors; one tavern was named The Giant Saloon, the other The Goliath House. A very lively carriage trade developed to carry train passengers from the station to Newell's and back again. The hotel in Cardiff was packed with paying customers, as was just about every farmhouse in the area with a spare room or couch. One clever manufacturer even found a way to use the Cardiff Giant in his advertisements:

"The proprietors of the Stone Giant think they will have to take his giantship out of his pit . . . before long, for it's growing cold, and they're afraid he'll freeze." The answer to this dilemma? Simple: purchase "The Oriental base burning heating furnace, sold at Pease, Johnson & Plaisted, 77 South Salina, Syracuse."

Newell and his partners may have been the ones making the big money, but it seemed that everybody in Cardiff was trying to benefit economically from the giant's presence.

Attendance at the Newell farm dropped off slightly following the crush on Sunday, the result of very bad weather and the obligations of work. But giant fever was still in full swing in newspapers everywhere as hundreds of people offered their opinions on the subject.

The vast majority of folk still felt the giant was a petrified person. A University of Rochester professor believed this but offered as his only evidence the fact that his friend the Reverend E. F. Owen did, too: "It is the opinion of Mr. Owen, and indeed of most scientific men who have given it an examination, that it is a petrified human body." Some concocted a "scientific" explanation for why petrifaction could happen, such as local doctor Ashbil Searle. He was confident that a combination of cold underground water and "wet alluvial oil" had speeded up fossilization so much that the body had no chance to rot. Still others pointed to the thousands of fossilized plants, tree trunks, insects, and fish already unearthed and asked, "Will any one say that under favorable circumstances a fossil man cannot be formed?"

But the biggest reason cited for petrifaction was the giant himself. His immense size, the look on his face all spoke to people of the distant past. One visiting minister was quoted by Andrew White as saying, "Is it not strange that any human being, after seeing the wonderfully preserved figure, can deny the evidence of his senses, and refuse to believe . . . that we have here a fossilized human being, perhaps one of the giants mentioned in Scripture?"

Of course, the statue theory had its

advocates. Contrary to popular belief, most scientists believed the Cardiff Giant was man-made. Boynton came back for a second examination and exclaimed, "It is positively absurd to consider this a 'fossil man.'" Archaeologist Wills De Hass proclaimed it a statue and wondered, "May not a wandering sculptor have penetrated the Valley of the Onondaga or a wave of more advanced civilization settled here in pre-historic times." While former New York State Geologist and then Director of the New York State Museum of Natural History, James Hall, was adamant that "the Giant . . . is a statue. . . ."

Yet all of these esteemed scientists proclaimed the giant to be ancient and an important find. Boynton's no-nonsense voice turned downright reverential when he admitted, "The statue, being colossal and massive, strikes the beholder with a feeling of awe. . . . [It] is one of the greatest curiosities of the early history of Onondaga county. . . ." Hall took this a step further, saying, "Altogether, it is the most remarkable object yet brought to light in our country, and . . . deserving of the attention of archeologists."

Whatever side of the debate a person was on, the fact that citizens and scientists alike found the Cardiff Giant a true marvel was extremely satisfying. The giant linked the present inhabitants of the United States to a distant and inspiring past, one that might even rival the cultures of ancient Egypt, Greece, and Rome. In a very real way, it allowed the people of a young and unsophisticated country to feel they were on an equal footing with their older, more established European counterparts. As the *Commercial Advertiser* pointed out, "The Syracuse people hold their heads higher than ever now that their ancestors are found to be so imposing."

But Newell wasn't thinking about the origin of the giant or what it might mean to his neighbors or the country. Unpleasant questions were being asked about the giant's authenticity, and Newell was trying to figure out how to answer them.

VI.
EMBARRASSING ACCUSATIONS

Not everyone was convinced that the giant (whether petrified or sculpted) was a true antique. James Lawrence, an experienced, hard-nosed Syracuse lawyer, visited the giant and wrote an accusing letter that was published in a local newspaper. In it, he pointed a suspicious finger at Newell and demanded to know why he needed a second well when the first one was still working just fine. He also noted that the farmer had only two cows and a horse to water.

Why exactly did he want a second well? And wasn't it a little too convenient that Newell had made sure he had a lot of workers there as witnesses, picked the precise spot of the well, and instructed those workers to dig down four feet? "Why, all this show and parade," Lawrence asked in concluding his case, "unless to cover up the real object, viz: finding a treasure?"

Other rumors then began to circulate in the newspapers. Cardiff hotel owner Avery Fellows remembered putting up a man named George Hull at his establishment a year earlier. He also recalled driving Hull over to a spot near Newell's farm. Hull was a particularly easy man to remember. At six feet three, he towered over almost everyone else, had slicked-back hair and a big, bushy mustache, and often wore a long, black coat that flapped dramatically in a breeze. But it was his eyes that mesmerized and intimidated folk. "Those eyes looked right at us," a man who knew Hull remembered, "and seemed to pry . . . and cork-screw their way clear down into the innermost recesses of our souls."

Even if he hadn't been physically memorable, people wouldn't have forgotten him. The forty-eight-year-old Hull had a long and shady past that included being a quick-talking horse trader and the inventor of a new sort of marked playing cards, which he had tested out on unsuspecting folk in the area. He was also thought to be related to Newell, though no one knew whether this was actually true.

Mention of Hull brought forth reports that several people had seen him a year earlier traveling through local villages by wagon. The wagon was being drawn by four very large, very powerful horses, and carried an oversize iron-bound box. The box, folk insisted, had been big enough to have contained the giant.

At first, newspapers printed these rumors without saying whether or not they believed them. But editorials did point out that western New York had had a number of extremely unusual people and odd situations that had cropped up in the past. The *New York Herald* reminded readers that Joseph Smith, the founder of the Latter-day Saints, had claimed to have been led by an angel to a site not many miles from Cardiff, where he found golden plates. Smith insisted they were a holy book written in an ancient language that only he could read, using two small stones given to him by the angel. Smith's beliefs were strongly criticized by the outspoken and openly anti-Mormon essayist Ezra C. Seaman who called Smith's religion "the grossest, foulest, and most corrupting imposture which has been successfully imposed upon a people. . . ."

Other papers pointed out that the region was also the birthplace of the

It was also home to the Fox sisters, two young girls who, in 1848, insisted they could communicate with the dead. Both Miller and the Fox sisters had amassed a very large and enthusiastic following.

And then there was the Silver Lake Monster that terrorized the area in the mid-1850s. It turned out that a Silver Lake hotel owner, Artemus Walker, had constructed a sixty-foot-long snake from wire and waterproof canvas with glowing red eyes and a wide-open mouth filled with long, sharp fangs. Walker towed his creation around the lake at night to alarm residents and (he hoped) to boost tourism. His prank had worked very nicely for two very profitable summer seasons before being exposed. Looking at the region's history, the *New York Sun* ridiculed Cardiff resi-

The Fox sisters Maggie (left) and Kate (center) claimed that rapping sounds were how dead souls communicated with the living. Leah (right) would later manage her sisters' careers as mediums.

Millerites. The group had been founded by William Miller, who had claimed the world would end in 1843 (and when it didn't, the date was moved to 1844 and then 1845).

dents for being so gullible and added, "Western New York is, for some unaccountable reason, a permanent hotbed for the growth of all sorts of humbugs."

As if to strike a fatal blow to the Cardiff Giant story, another letter to the *Herald* claimed to reveal the true tale. The letter was signed "Thomas B. Ellis, a resident of Syracuse." Ellis reported that a dying local quarryman, George Hooker, became friends with a strange hermit named Jules Geraud. Geraud was also in failing health, but Hooker insisted that he had seen a statue of a giant man that Geraud was chiseling in his wood cabin. Geraud's cabin burned down shortly after his death and the statue was never found, but Hooker swore that Newell's giant was "the same statue found lying in the cabin of Jules Geraud." These new claims prompted the *Herald* to run a boldfaced headline that announced the Cardiff Giant to be "A STUPENDOUS HOAX."

Newell denied the rumors and even swore out an affidavit that he had no knowledge of the giant before its discovery. All of the men who had been there when the giant was discovered did the same, swearing that they had seen nothing unusual at the farm, except the giant itself. Newell also revealed that he had signed a new clause to his partnership agreement. It stated that if the giant was proved to be a fake within three months, he would return all of the money given to him and forfeit the money still owed.

Most newspapers and most people were impressed that Newell and the other men had sworn they were telling the absolute truth. Apparently, they weren't concerned that because they hadn't done this in a court of law it had absolutely no legal standing whatsoever. They also felt that the fraud clause showed that Newell was a man of pure intentions.

Meanwhile, Hull appeared in town and explained that he had indeed been in the area a year before, but was there to ship machinery on the railroad. He was even able to produce a receipt from the railroad company as proof.

Finally, sentiment in favor of Newell grew stronger when it was revealed that the Geraud story was actually an elaborate practical joke. A person identified only as "W" confessed that he'd done it because he disliked all the attention Cardiff and its resident giant were getting.

The American Goliah pamphlet also addressed the issue of a hoax in a section labeled: "Is There Any Fraud or Deception?" Its answer is self-serving, of course, but rang true for the vast majority of people. "It has the marks of the ages stamped upon every limb and feature," it states with authority. "I have not seen the first person who entertained any doubt of its great antiquity. . . ."

The *Syracuse Daily Journal* then reaffirmed its belief that the giant was a true antiquity, citing the views of all the scientists who had examined it. It finished by praising Newell and saying, "His good character, the circumstances of the discovery, and the evidence open to the public scrutiny, contradict these rumors." Other newspapers followed suit, with the *Daily Standard* condemning anyone who made up or spread such nasty rumors as "lacking greatly in the upper story."

Ordinary people also came to the giant's defense. One letter writer to the *Daily Courier* identified only as F.C.W. weighed in with "As I have looked upon this wonderful object, I will give you my first impressions, which I believe, are those of nine-tenths of the people who look upon him, viz: that the object before me was once a living human being." People, Andrew White pointed out, had a "joy in believing" and "came to abhor any doubts regarding the Cardiff Giant."

After producing his receipt and declaring he had nothing to do with the Cardiff Giant, George Hull slipped out of town and away from the limelight. Newell repeatedly declared that his giant was genuine and even had his new business partners invite more scientists in to study it. The suggestions that the Cardiff Giant was a complete humbug never completely went away, but the initial wave of doubt passed and the show went on.

The ugly truth was that Stub Newell was a bold-faced liar!

VII.
THE UGLY TRUTH

Yes, Stub Newell *was* lying! But he wasn't as big a liar as George Hull. Hull had the unique ability to look a person straight in the eyes and say convincingly that he was being absolutely honest when in truth he was stealing the person blind. Newell, on the other hand, was beginning to feel that time was running out, and that he might well be charged with fraud. He never confessed openly, but his actions spoke volumes. He secretly put his farm up for sale and began preparing to move away from Cardiff.

What exactly was the truth?

Hull claimed that he got the idea to create the giant in 1867 while on a business trip to Ackley, Iowa. While there, he met and began talking about the Bible with a saddlebag preacher named Henry B. Turk. Turk was, in Hull's words, "an earnest and a zealous worker in the Lord's vineyard" who believed every word in the Bible was one hundred percent accurate. Hull, an avowed nonbeliever, took the preacher to task on a number of issues, especially regarding the existence of

George Hull as he appeared several years after the Cardiff Giant hoax.

giants. It was, Hull remembered, "a long discussion and a hot one."

Hull attacked as absurd the notion that giants once existed. Turk held firm, saying, "I believe there were giants. I don't know how big, but the Bible says that Og's bedstead was nine cubits long and four cubits broad [so] I suppose that he was fifteen or sixteen feet [tall]."

Their argument went on for several hours, with Turk finally stating that "We have to believe these things, they are in the Good Book." Hull was just as adamant, and went to bed that night with his mind churning over the conversation. "I lay awake wondering why people would believe those remarkable stories in the Bible about giants when suddenly I thought of making a stone giant, and passing it off as a petrified man."

Hull was in many ways a common criminal, but he was also clever and reasonably well-read. He had studied Charles Darwin's *On the Origin of Species* and followed discussions of his controversial theory about evolution in the newspapers. He'd also attended lectures and read a number of books on fossils and geology.

Like many people at the time, Hull was fascinated by all branches of the sciences — whether it was how engineers designed and lay down the transatlantic telegraph cable or what archaeologists were discovering about ancient civilizations around the world. People were interested and eager to learn as much as possible. "We live in the midst of a general and high development of knowledge," the Reverend Benjamin Martin said in a lecture, "the age is scientific." And Hull was happy to cash in on this collective desire to know more.

He also understood that people could be fooled if the object looked authentic enough and was "discovered" and presented in a believable way. He found examples of this in the numerous private museums around the country then being operated by people like Joseph Wood and P. T. Barnum. These places were filled to the brim with real and phony "wonders of the world." Hull knew about and admired one of Barnum's most famous frauds from the past, the Feejee Mermaid.

In 1842, Barnum bought a three-foot-long shriveled carcass that was human-like above the waist and had the fin and tail of a fish below. To create interest in his mermaid before actually presenting it to the public, Barnum wrote a series of bogus letters to New York City newspapers about a certain Dr. Griffin who had made many wonderful discoveries during his world travels. Naturally, this also included the preserved remains of a real mermaid.

Barnum then hired a friend to play the part of Dr. Griffin, who gave a learned lecture on mermaids. The paying public and newspapers ate up Griffin's talk, with one paper proclaiming "Mermaid Is World's Most Fascinating Discovery!!!" As cultural historian John Kasson noted, "Americans [at the time] were easy targets for anything couched in blandly neutral scientific and technological language."

Today, specialists who are experts in marine biology and anatomy would be

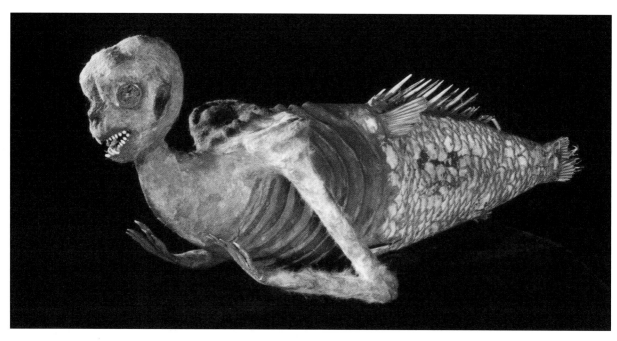

The Feejee Mermaid as it appears today.

brought in to examine such a find and decide whether or not it was real. But few people who claimed to be "specialists" back in 1869 actually possessed a deep knowledge of the subjects. Prehistoric archaeology was a fairly new field of study at the time. Harvard University wouldn't award a graduate degree in prehistoric archaeology until 1894. In addition, universities were only just beginning to offer graduate degrees in such subjects as geology, general archaeology, and paleontology. Hull knew he could use this general lack of knowledge, plus Americans' love of science, to manipulate people into seeing what he wanted them to see. But to fool the public, he would first have to create a truly "real" giant.

Hull realized that to create a stone giant would require a very large block of stone and a skilled sculptor, and that both would cost more money than he had. After a brief search, he came upon Henry Martin, a successful black-smith and inventor. Hull told Martin about his scheme and made him an equal partner in exchange for cash to cover half the giant's expense. Hull got the other half of the required money by burning down two of his own cigar businesses and collecting the insurance.

After several months of scouting suitable stone quarries, Martin found the perfect material from which to fashion a giant: Fort Dodge (Iowa) gypsum. This particular gypsum was abundant and fairly inexpensive; it was also soft and easily carved. Hull and Martin ran into a problem when a prominent Fort Dodge quarry owner took a disliking to them and refused to cut them a huge block of gypsum. It seemed as if the scheme was at a dead end when Hull learned about a Chicago marble dealer named Edward Burkhardt.

Burkhardt was used to handling large and very heavy slabs of quarried material. He had the skilled workers who could excavate and transport the stone and had contacts with a number of sculptors. Burkhardt liked the idea of producing a giant sculpture and making money from it, so he agreed to help as long as he was made an equal partner and as long as he was paid his regular fees for any work he did.

At the end of June, the three men rented an acre of land in Fort Dodge and set a team of workers digging and cutting out their gypsum block. The 6,560-pound slab was loaded onto a sturdy army wagon and slowly hauled forty miles to a railroad station in Montana, where it was shipped to Chicago. Burkhardt then brought in marble cutter Frederick Mohrmann as well as his assistant, Henry Salle, to design a clay model of a giant and sculpt it. Both Mohrmann and Salle were paid a flat fee for their labors, with a promise of more money once the scheme began paying off.

With Hull, Martin, and Burkhardt advising (and Hull actually posing for the sculpture), Mohrmann and Salle went to work. Eighteen days later they presented the partners with a giant. This first version sported curly hair on the giant's head, which Hull had removed. Hull had learned from his various readings that hair could never be fossilized.

"On the under side of the body I cut away some places," Hull told a reporter years later, "as I did not wish to have the giant too perfect, because there should be some parts of his flesh which had not

A mule-drawn wagon filled with chunks of gypsum, the material from which Hull's giant was made.

petrified and therefore rotted away." He further aged his creation by having the cutters sand it head to toe to make it look worn, colored it with blue ink, and then washed the entire surface with sulfuric acid. A final, creative touch was to pound knitting needles through a piece of wood and whack the giant all over to create tiny pores in the skin.

Once aged to perfection, Hull and company had to find a spot to bury and unearth their giant. The key was to locate a place where fossils were common so that finding the giant would not seem so unusual or odd. Places were considered in Connecticut, Massachusetts, and even Mexico. Finally, Hull suggested that somewhere in western New York State might be the best place because, as Hull recalled, "Geologists say it was at one time a lake, and many petrified fish and reptiles have been found there. . . ."

On September 24, 1868, the statue — now weighing 3,720 pounds — departed Chicago via the railroad in an iron-bound box headed for New York State. While waiting for it to arrive, Hull visited sev-eral villages trying to find the best location. In the end, he decided that Stub Newell's farm was just about perfect. Newell, eager to make a buck, was brought in as an equal partner, and Hull arranged to have the giant transported there.

Hull next hired two men, one being a twenty-one-year-old relative, to move the boxed giant by wagon to Newell's farm. It was during this journey that Hull stayed in Cardiff and had hotel owner Avery Fellows drop him off near the farm. It was also when the wagon was spotted by curious residents as it crept along back roads and through little villages on the way to Cardiff.

Hull and his two drivers arrived at night and stored the giant in Newell's barn, covering it completely with straw and hay. They returned a week later to bury their creation. By prearrangement, Newell and his family were away visiting relatives, and Hull and the other men were able to work undetected during the following seven nights. After the giant was in the ground and the hole filled in, Hull spread clover seed on the bare dirt.

As with all of the others involved, the drivers were paid well for their help and promised more money later (as long as they kept their participation in the scheme a secret).

The men packed some machinery Newell had left behind in the barn in another metal box, and Hull had it shipped off, carefully pocketing the receipt. The larger iron-bound box was destroyed and everyone returned home to wait. Hull calculated that the entire scheme had cost almost $3,000 ($48,700).

He was desperate for cash at the time, but he knew he would have to be patient if the deception was to work. And so, the giant would rest in the wet soil until a full year passed and it was time to unearth him.

This is the shortened version of the creation, transportation, and burial of the Cardiff Giant. In *The Giantmaker*, Hull insisted he pulled the hoax to tweak the noses of people who took the Bible to be literally true. Despite this claim, it's clear that at the center of his deception were a monumental ego and a craving for big money.

Newell added another layer of deception to the scheme by failing to tell his new business partners from Syracuse that Hull or anyone else was involved or that the remaining twenty-five percent interest in the giant was being split. To do this would be to admit that the giant was a fraud and obligate him to repay the money he'd received.

Newell's six new partners were indeed nervous that the giant might be a fake. That was why it was they (and not Newell) who had insisted that Newell add a fraud clause to the original partnership agreement and asked that several other experts view the giant. But they never really bothered to look very deeply into the issue. After all, experts like Boynton and Hall had already called the statue a genuine ancient artifact, not once but twice. Besides, they were already looking to the future for even greater profits.

VIII.
A GIANT MOVE

To maintain their healthy flow of money, they decided to take their giant on a national tour. They planned to begin by exhibiting it in Syracuse, followed by visits to a list of cities that would include Albany, New York City, Boston, Philadelphia, New Orleans, Chicago, and even San Francisco.

But before they took the show on the road, a new group of esteemed scientists, doctors, judges, and ministers came to examine the giant one more time. On Wednesday, November 3, this group looked over the giant very carefully and came to a unanimous conclusion: It was a legitimate antique. As one paper put it: "For the present, it must suffice for us to know that the charges of [fraud] were utterly rejected by the investigators."

Two days later, on Friday, November 5,

the tent and fence were removed and a derrick was erected over the giant's pit. In addition to a large group of observers, Calvin O. Gott was there to take the very first official photographs of the great wonder.

At around 11:30 in the morning, a specially hired crew hauled away on the heavy ropes, and the pulley wheel began to squeak. Slowly, slowly, the giant emerged from his muddy grave until he was dangling four and a half feet above

The Cardiff Giant being lifted from his watery grave.

the lip of the pit. The work was halted briefly while Gott staged another photograph, which was followed by a rousing cheer from those assembled.

Thick boards were placed over the pit and a wagon driven in under the giant. Finally, the workers lowered the giant into a large box filled with sand. Later, a local humorist penned this little rhyme:

> *Take him up tenderly,*
> *Move him with care,*
> *Doing no harm,*
> *For he's worth more to-day,*
> *Than Stub Newell's farm.*

The giant was taken to a factory in Syracuse where he was cleaned and weighed. On Saturday morning, he was paraded through the streets of Syracuse followed by an estimated one thousand cheering citizens and a marching band. Newspapers noted that the band played "See, the Conquering Hero Comes." Eventually, the parade ended at Shakespeare Hall, which had a large exhibition arcade.

Colonel Joseph H. Wood had been hard at work on the space to have it ready for a Monday opening. The giant was placed in the center of the room on an eight-inch-high pedestal. A railing was constructed around him with richly designed fabric draped over it. A six-foot-tall platform was built around three sides of the giant and a mirror was placed behind him so viewers could see his arm behind his back. Because the show was much grander than the one at Newell's farm, the owners increased the entrance charge to one dollar.

Visitors would first walk along the platform, seeing the stone wonder from above. They would then descend the stairs to stand in front of him for a closer examination. After just a few minutes, ushers would escort them out of the room to make way for the next group.

The Monday opening was an instant hit, with over 1,000 people paying to catch a brief glimpse of the discovery. Attendance increased all week long, with Saturday seeing 2,000 paying customers come through the doors. Attendance would average between 1,500 and 2,000 a day, but over 4,000 eager customers lined up to see the giant on the day after Thanksgiving. So many people were traveling to see the wondrous discovery, that the New York Central Railroad had trains stop for ten minutes near the

An oversize wagon had to be built to haul the Cardiff Giant to Syracuse.

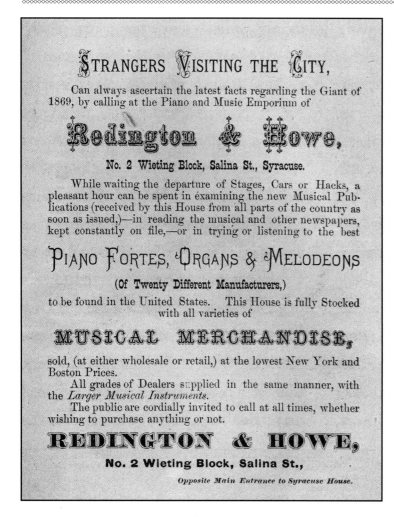

The owners of the Redington & Howe music store placed this ad in The American Goliah, *hoping to attract some of the curious tourists to their store.*

hall so riders could run in for a quick view. By November 26, when the giant was shipped off to its next engagement in Albany, somewhere between 35,000 and 40,000 people had visited the Cardiff Giant.

Hull would later admit that even he was surprised at how enormously popular his giant had become. He had no way of knowing it, but the giant had touched a deep emotional nerve in a vast number of Americans.

The United States and Europe were experiencing what historians have come to call the Industrial Revolution. Basically, coal-fueled steam engines allowed businesses to manufacture a wide variety of goods with automated machines. This in turn created a need for more and more factory workers, which resulted in the growth of cities near manufacturing facilities.

But as cities grew in size and importance, rural towns and villages began to shrink and farms began to disappear. People still living in these places felt left behind, and wondered if they would have any sort of significant future, if in fact they mattered at all to the country at large. "The future having failed to give them hope of relevance," cultural historian John Kasson explained, "townspeople turned to the past to assert themselves and their way of life."

An increasing number of small towns established historical societies that published books and pamphlets; they also staged commemorations to honor and celebrate past events and significant individuals. The discovery of the Cardiff Giant in a rural village fed into this desire to be relevant and important. "[The giant] had the potential to establish Cardiff as the cradle of the American nation," Kasson reasoned. And with it, all other small towns and villages felt their status elevated as well because no one knew what other wonders were yet to be discovered.

The six new partners didn't really care what emotional needs their giant satisfied. They just knew that the swarms of customers meant that they had already earned well over their original investment of $30,000. And they still had many lucrative stops to come. One of these partners was particularly pleased. Newell's friend William Spencer managed to sell half of his one-eighth share, which originally cost him $1,250 ($20,300), to a Utica merchant named Benjamin Son for the tidy sum of $5,000 ($81,200).

Stub Newell was probably the happiest giant owner as he left Syracuse. He had unloaded the remaining quarter share of the giant he held with Hull, Martin, and Burkhardt to thirty-four-year-old John Rankin, a businessman and future mayor of Binghamton. The price was a cool $25,000 ($406,000), almost all of it in bank notes that would be paid off at a later date. So as not to raise any suspicions and cast further doubts on the giant, Newell and Rankin kept the deal a secret.

The giant's owners and former owners might have been less self-satisfied if they knew that other men had secrets of their own. And that those secrets were aimed at undercutting everything they had so carefully built up.

IX.
ENTER BARNUM

On Monday morning, December 6, a strange procession made its way up Broadway in New York City. The mini-parade was composed of a single wagon carrying a huge iron box being pulled by twelve massive Flanders horses. Flanking the wagon were one hundred colorfully dressed hired marchers. Crowds soon lined the sidewalks and word began to spread: The Cardiff Giant had come to town. This impression was reinforced by a sign attached to the side of the box that read: "The Petrified Giant for Wood's Museum."

But this wasn't a museum owned by the Colonel Wood who had staged the giant's homes at Newell's farm and in Syracuse. It was instead George Wood's place, and this Wood was a business partner of the nationally known showman P. T. Barnum.

Initially, Barnum had said he wasn't interested in making an offer on the real Cardiff Giant. But as the days turned to weeks and the giant managed to stay in the headlines, Barnum became more and more intrigued. Late in November, Barnum slipped into Syracuse to see "his stone majesty."

Barnum was impressed and thought it "the greatest marvel of the age." He then got down to business, offering $50,000 ($812,000) for a quarter interest

P. T. Barnum posed for this photograph with his "man in miniature," General Tom Thumb.

to Newell (who was still believed to own a portion of the giant) and the other new owners of the giant.

This was a very substantial offer, but the giant's owners took only a few minutes to reject it. Barnum would up the offer several times, but the partnership said no again and again. Part of their reasoning was that the giant was attracting large crowds all by itself, so they really didn't need the master showman's skills to draw an audience. A few of the men, lead by Amos Westcott, did not want Barnum's soiled reputation as a humbug artist to sully either the giant's or their good names.

While Barnum did not get to possess the giant, he didn't leave Syracuse empty-handed. He had been following the goings-on in Cardiff closely by reading newspaper reports and had come across an article about a local sculptor's attempt to duplicate the giant. Those who believed the giant was a petrified human insisted that no sculptor could create such a lifelike statue. "[Carl Franz Otto] was led to make this attempt," the *Daily Journal* explained, "[after] hearing it asserted that such a thing could not be done."

After Otto visited the giant several times and studied the recently taken Gott photographs, he made a large clay model. Following this, he made a cast of the model, then he filled it with plaster of paris, marble dust, and other pieces of small stone. When it was dry, he colored his giant blue-gray and began to age it. Even before being completely finished, a newspaper pronounced that Otto's "imitation of the original is very perfect."

Barnum was impressed by the imitation giant and began negotiating with Otto to purchase it. Because Otto had gotten himself into legal trouble by selling his giant to several different people at the same time, Barnum began by offering to pay off these claims. Otto was finally persuaded to sell when Barnum said he would pay him $100 ($1,620) a week for three months and put him up free of charge at a fancy New York City hotel. The deal done and signed, Otto's giant was shipped to its new home in New York City.

Both Barnum and Wood were big-time showmen who aimed to awe and impress citizens in order to entice them to their museum. Their December 6 parade was meant to get the city's attention in a big way, and it succeeded. Even before they officially opened their exhibit, newspaper editors flocked to the museum for a private viewing of the discovery. Hull later claimed that they had paid off reporters to get good reviews, and it's possible that some bribes were accepted. Several papers were always kind to Barnum even after it was clear that his giant was not the original.

Barnum and Wood also flooded the city with advertisements. An ad in the *New York Daily Tribune* announced: "A MOST IMPRESSIVE MYSTERY! THE PHENOMENON OF THE CENTURY, THE STONE MAN OF ONONDAGA!" They challenged people to come to the museum to decide the ultimate question: "Is it a Statue? Is it a Petrifaction? Is it a Stupen-dous Fraud? Is it the Remains of a former Race?"

When the doors opened on Monday, several hundred people braved cold winds and icy rain to see this new giant. It was displayed in the center of the exhibit space on a raised, pyramid-shaped pedestal. Dark green globes covered the gas jets, creating dim, solemn lighting, much like the interior of a cathedral. The railings and woodwork were draped in thick black cloth and the ushers wore slippers to maintain the somber quiet.

The New York City newspapers quickly noted that there seemed to be two Cardiff Giants, with several referring to the Barnum-Wood giant in a positive way as a "colossus" and a "distinguished visitor." The *New York Herald* took a decidedly more negative stance when it said: "We forbear to distinguish between these giants or to decide which is the greater of two humbugs." Meanwhile the *New York Commercial Advertiser* took a middle ground that still managed to promote the Barnum giant, suggesting that "truth is mighty and must prevail. . . . Between these two [giants] the public, which pays its money, is at full liberty to make its choice."

Whatever the public felt about the giant (be it a petrifaction, an ancient statue, or an utter fraud), they came in droves. And with an entrance charge of only thirty cents, they seem to have gotten a genuine bargain since they could also wander around the museum to see its many other wonders and oddities.

Seeing their giant challenged so boldly and successfully (and their future profits imperiled), the owners of the "real" Cardiff Giant decided they had to act. They rushed to New York Supreme Court to file an injunction to stop the Barnum exhibition. Ironically, the injunction wound up being heard by Judge George Barnard.

If anything, Barnard was a bigger fraud than either of the giants. He had been appointed a judge by the notoriously corrupt William M. "Boss" Tweed even though Barnard knew nothing about the law. His own brother said Barnard was about as smart as a "yellow dog" when it came to his legal judgments.

Barnard always made rulings in favor of Tweed and his cronies. He granted citizenship to thousands of immigrants with the provision that they all vote for Tweed's handpicked candidates in future elections. He was also known to drink brandy and whittle while testimony was being given in his court.

In the case of giant vs. giant, Barnard interrupted the Cardiff Giant's lawyers well before they had finished reading their documents. He said there was probably no reason *not* to grant the injunction to close Barnum's exhibit, but that "he had been doing a great deal of injunctions lately, and felt disposed to 'Shut down'" for a rest. He summarily dismissed the case, adding that "he was not inclined to interfere [in] a fight between Cardiff Giants." When the Cardiff Giant's lawyers protested, Barnard quieted them with "Bring your giant here, and if he swears to his genuineness as a *bona fide* petrifaction, you shall have the injunction."

Having lost their case and seeing profits continue to go to Barnum and Wood, the owners of the Cardiff Giant attacked the impostor by calling it "a plaster cast taken from the original by Mr. Otto . . . without our knowledge and consent." They then touted the authenticity of their giant by stating,

William "Boss" Tweed (right) shakes hands with newspaper publisher Horace Greeley. Many people believed that Tweed paid Greeley to write favorable articles about him.

"The Cardiff giant is now at the State Geological Hall, in Albany, where a room was placed at our disposal by the authorities of the State." They also promised to bring the real giant to New York City in the very near future.

Barnum and Wood fired back, stating that if anyone could prove their giant was a plaster cast taken from the Cardiff Giant, they would happily donate $1,000

($16,200) to the New York Association for Improving the Condition of the Poor. They also had one of Barnum's assistants issue a sworn statement that the Barnum-Wood giant was indeed a carved statue. As with Stub Newell's earlier sworn statement, the assistant's carried absolutely no legal weight.

The dispute played out in the newspapers, which only increased attendance for the Barnum-Wood giant. People continued to visit the statue even after the newspapers seemed to have tired of the entire story. One Philadelphia paper said, "It is rather rich that we should be victimized by such a fraud upon a fraud."

The owners of the original Cardiff Giant had no choice but to box up their man and get him to New York City as quickly as possible. On December 20, they set him up at a site that was only two blocks from Wood's Museum. Everything had been done so hastily that the room wasn't even decorated to enhance the viewing experience of the public. Still, the two giants were now ready to duel it out for the public's attention. Or as the *Commercial Advertiser* put it: "Two men of gypsum are in town, each claiming to be the original Cardiff wonder. . . . By and by they may come to blows, and then the consequences will be fearful to contemplate."

In the end, it turned out to be no contest. The first day attendance for the original Cardiff Giant was described as "fair" by a newspaper and probably numbered two or three hundred. The next day, he drew only fifty visitors. Meanwhile, the Barnum-Wood giant continued to pull in record-sized crowds, with over 5,000 visitors on Christmas Day. The *New York Sun* quickly called the winner: "Barnum has thus completely triumphed. He has checkmated the opposition completely and routed them ignominiously."

Barnum had once again proved that he was the absolute master of humbug. But even as he celebrated his victory and counted his profits, the complete undoing of his giant and the original Cardiff Giant was in the works.

X.
GIANT PROBLEMS ALL AROUND

The downfall of the twin giants began well before the duel in New York City, with a simple letter from Fillmore Smith that reached several Syracuse newspapers at the end of October 1869. Smith was a twenty-four-year-old mining engineer who explained that gypsum would dissolve fairly quickly in the water-soaked ground on Newell's farm. He ended by adding, "We are thus reduced to the necessity of believing that the statue has been placed there within a very recent period — say one or two years."

Smith's letter and reasoning were largely ignored by the general public and the newspapers. One letter writer scoffed, "Now let me ask, do not all the scientific men who have made an examination of this wonderful object [say that] it is of great antiquity . . . ?"

But at least one person took Smith's letter to heart: John Boynton. Boynton read the letter with growing alarm as he worried he'd been completely duped. He immediately began an experiment by running water over a one-pound piece of gypsum; it dissolved completely within twenty-four hours. Not only did Boynton confirm Smith's conclusions, he was able to say that the Cardiff Giant had been buried approximately 370 days before it was "discovered" by the well-diggers.

An embarrassed Boynton wrote to the director of the Smithsonian Institution about his findings, adding that "my veneration for the high antiquity of the Onondaga Giant is fast waning to a taper." He promised to do more research and to make his conclusions public.

Boynton was moving very cautiously and slowly here. If he had indeed been suckered into believing the carving was ancient, it would be a major blow to his professional reputation. But if he claimed it was a fraud and was wrong about that . . . well, he would be the laughing-stock of his scientific peers and the public. Yet despite the risks, he did send a copy of this letter to two newspapers, where it appeared on November 17.

Very few people bothered to listen to him, even after he attacked the giant in a public lecture. The Geraud story had already been proved a hoax, and Newell had been praised as straightforward and honest. No one was in the mood for more anti-giant talk. The *Daily Standard* reported, "The Doctor frankly confessed that he had changed his views as to some things in regard to the Giant, and it was quite evident he is down on Old Gypsum." But the paper refused to print his entire lecture, so very few readers were persuaded that he was correct.

The *Worcester Spy* was downright dismissive: "Dr. Boynton [is] not a high authority, [and] has given up the hypothesis which he first used to explain the mystery. . . . His reasons, however, are not satisfactory; for the soft gypsum used in his experiments is not like the material of which the statue is made." Once again, the fact that most of the proclaimed experts weren't really expert in their respective fields played into Hull's hands.

It wasn't until late in November that noted paleontologist O. C. Marsh paid the Cardiff Giant a visit. Marsh had studied paleontology in Europe and returned to the United States where he was appointed professor of paleontology

Fossil hunting was a rough, dangerous business back in the nineteenth century. Here O. C. Marsh (center back row) is surrounded by his well-armed research assistants.

by Yale University in 1866. He had also studied mineralogy, natural history, and geology. During his extensive studies, he had been taught to examine and question objects in great detail. For instance, Marsh noticed immediately that the statue's chisel marks had been made by modern tools and not from the kinds of tools used hundreds of years before.

Marsh examined the statue for a few minutes and came to the same conclusion as Smith and Boynton; the Cardiff Giant was "of very recent origin, and a most decided humbug." Marsh also attacked the scientists who had authenticated the giant as an ancient artifact, saying, "I am surprised that any scientific observer should not have at once detected the unmistakable evidence against its antiquity."

This was followed a few days later by the first reports from citizens of Fort Dodge, Iowa, regarding the origin of the gypsum. Galusha Parsons saw the giant during its stay in Syracuse and wrote back to his hometown newspaper, "I believe [the Cardiff Giant] is made of that great block of gypsum those fellows got at Fort Dodge a year ago." The Iowa papers began running a series of articles tracing the movements of Hull and Martin, with one citizen even recalling Hull's name.

Clearly, evidence was mounting against Hull and his giant, and Hull was growing increasingly nervous. Not so much at being found out. He was actually rather proud of what he had accomplished and wanted people to know he was the mastermind of the entire scheme. But he was worried that the fraud would be officially proven before January 24. That was when the three-month time period in the fraud clause ran out and Hull and his three other original partners would be able to legally collect all the money still owed them.

Out of desperation, Hull approached Ezra Walrath, the former editor of the most outspoken anti–Cardiff Giant newspaper, the *Daily Courier*. Hull had a proposition for Walrath. Hull would tell him the entire story of the giant if Walrath promised not to print any details that would establish fraud before the

January date. He also said he would let Walrath coauthor his book about the Cardiff Giant and share in its profits. Like the twenty other men already involved in the giant scheme, Walrath smelled money and agreed to the deal.

Walrath did give out certain vague details to friends at the paper, and an article appeared in the *Daily Courier* saying that "a certain person" had "made a full confession of the birth, origin, life and history of the giant." Another newspaper revealed that the statue had been carved in Chicago. Meanwhile, the *Daily Standard* announced that Newell was in the process of selling his farm and moving from the area, which the paper took as a clear sign of a guilty conscience.

Additional accusations continued to surface all through December. The new owners of the Cardiff Giant did their best to deny the charges, but even they were beginning to believe the worst. By early January 1870, they felt their giant was a recently made fraud and hired a lawyer to get their money back from Newell. They also decided to get their giant out of New York City and away from the far more popular Barnum-Wood giant.

The owners had other plans as well. One by one, they began selling off a part or all of their share of the giant to unsuspecting investors. The economic wisdom of this move was simple. An owner who had paid $5,000 ($81,200) for his original share could sell half of the share for the same amount. In this way, he couldn't lose any money, and could actually earn even more if people still kept coming to see the giant. The new owner, however, stood to lose everything if the fraud was exposed and the show closed too soon after the purchase.

And believe it or not, this was all perfectly legal at the time. The contracts the newest investors signed never promised that the giant was ancient or authentic. They said only that investors were buying a share in a stone giant and that they would receive a certain percentage of whatever profits might be earned. Because no lies were told in the contract, the new investors had no legal grounds to sue. It fell to the new investors to decide if the deal made sense, which is why the phrase "buyer beware" was so common back then.

Of course, while these deals were being made behind closed doors, other people were watching the giant wars and plotting in secret. In December, a third giant appeared in Utica, New York. A short time later, yet another imitation giant could be seen in Colonel Joseph Wood's Chicago Museum. It seems that sculptor Carl Otto decided he hadn't been treated fairly by Barnum and began manufacturing giants at a furious rate — and for sizable profits. Wood paid $3,000 ($48,700) for his, while the Utica businessman paid $5,000 ($81,200). Otto would eventually be commissioned to produce an additional seven giants. At least four other giants were manufactured by people other than Otto.

The original Cardiff Giant went from being a fascinating national story to a national joke in a matter of days. P. T. Barnum sensed the shift in the public mood and decided to get in on the action before the giant was history. He bought a second imitation giant and suggested that people come see "the two original Cardiff giants."

The real Cardiff Giant also acquired a new nickname. Now people began referring to him as "Old Hoaxy."

XI.
A GIANT FAREWELL

Even though most, if not all, of the owners of the original Cardiff Giant suspected it was a fake, they still wanted to make as much money as possible from it. Its arrival in Boston on January 22 was very subdued, with one newspaper saying only, "A big thing — the Cardiff Giant, at 113 Washington Street."

To get some needed publicity, the owners invited a prominent group of local intellectuals and scientists to a special viewing of the giant. One member of this delegation was the famous author Ralph Waldo Emerson. Emerson studied the giant from head to toe, then "with a microscope he repeated his inspection, and made himself . . . master of every feature and detail of the Giant." Asked what he thought about it, Emerson replied, "It is beyond the depth of my philosophy, very wonderful and undoubtedly ancient."

The entire group seemed to endorse the giant as truly ancient and therefore not a fraud. They did this knowing full well that many other people had condemned it as an artfully done hoax. Boston newspapers seem to have been swayed by the delegation's conclusions. The *Boston Morning Journal* said that "Our readers are familiar with its history and with the controversy that has arisen in regard to it. They have now a chance to decide whether it is a 'humbug' or not . . . We advise all to see it, for the leading question of the day will be, 'Have you seen the giant?'"

Some of the owners weighed in with passionate claims that the giant was indeed authentic. It seems that Hull, in a last-minute attempt to beat the fraud clause deadline, came forward with documents "proving" that the iron-bound box contained machinery and not the giant. Amos Westcott was so convinced that he exclaimed to the newspapers, "We now have ample proof that the fraud theories are without the least shadow of foundation in fact, and that these [hoax] theories are [themselves] the 'stupendous fraud and humbug.'" He also said that the rest of his partners had decided against invoking the fraud clause.

All of this positive publicity was enough to get the public's attention and draw in paying customers. The giant attracted between four hundred and a thousand people on its opening day. While it never drew the huge crowds of its early days, it did average a respectable five hundred visitors a day until May, when it finally left Boston for a tour of the Northeast.

By this time, the giant's reign as an authentic antiquity was essentially over. The two men who had carved the Cardiff Giant came forward to confess their role in the deception. They did not do this because of guilt or remorse; they did it because Hull had never bothered to pay them. His first partner, Henry Martin, did the same and for the same reason. Everyone was willing to remain quiet and go along with the deception as long as they stood a chance to profit by it. Once it was clear they were going to be cut out of the money, they decided to settle for a little revenge.

Many newspapers also sought a form of revenge for having been so completely bamboozled. Naturally, they took Hull and his fellow conspirators to task. The owner of the *New York Daily Tribune*, Horace Greeley, took a poke at Hull: "The behavior of Hull, in making a d — d fool of himself, is therefore to be deeply regretted." Greeley reserved his most sarcastic comments for the various men of science who had verified the giant's authenticity over and over again. "We of course understand that the eminent professors, geologists, antiquarians, and authorities on art and anatomy who vouched for the authenticity of the statue, are 'not up to small deceit or any sinful games,'" he said, adding, "but we should like to hear [some explanation] from these intelligent savants. . . ."

Greeley had conveniently forgotten that he and his paper had been a part of the deceit when they endorsed the giant and even defended it against those who were skeptical of its age. He wasn't alone in this. The *Albany Evening Journal* had called the giant "a remarkable find" and "astonishing" in October. By February, the paper demanded that State Geologist James Hall resign, calling him a "vulgar fraud" and nicknaming him "Dr. Fossil."

The giant continued his tour, visiting cities in Maine, Massachusetts, New York, Vermont, and Connecticut. Attendance declined until only a trickle of people were coming to see Old Hoaxy. Newspaper coverage such as that by the *Daily Journal* didn't help at all: "And who

is not tired of hearing of giants to the right of them, giants to the left of them? And who does not earnestly wish for the return of 'Jack, the giant-killer'?"

The owners and former owners of the Cardiff Giant agreed with this sentiment and simply wanted to get out without losing too much money. After numerous deals were made to transfer part ownership of the giant from one individual to another, a single man ended up owning the Cardiff Giant: none other than photographer Calvin Gott.

Gott did not want to abandon his photography business, so he turned the management of what remained of the Cardiff Giant tour over to storekeeper Billy Houghton. Houghton accompanied the giant on the last three official stops, then returned the statue to Gott's home in Fitchburg, Massachusetts, where it was stored in a shed with a leaky roof.

Gott tried to get other cities to host his giant, but none responded. To make what amounted to pocket change, Gott would haul his giant out of storage and take him to county fairs, where curious folk paid a nickel to see "the stone giant

John Rankin secretly owned a share of the Cardiff Giant and would later help George Hull write about the hoax.

that fooled the world." Gott later built a hotel with the express purpose of exhibiting the giant in the lobby to attract paying customers. While the building was under construction, Gott rented space in a nearby barn to store the giant.

Unfortunately, he ran out of money before the hotel could be finished. He then tried to sell the statue, but no one was willing to pay more than a modest amount. And so the Cardiff Giant was stuck in the barn until Gott died in 1890. The Cardiff Giant went to Gott's creditors, who turned out to be former owners of the giant, John Rankin and David Hannum.

They would eventually exhibit the giant at the 1901 Pan-American Exposition in Buffalo, New York, but it failed to excite much interest. The giant that had once intrigued scientists and citizens alike was brought back to Fitchburg, where he went into quiet retirement in the rented barn, his placid, stone smile fixed in place.

XII.
A FINAL RESTING PLACE

What happened to the major players in the Cardiff Giant hoax? Stub Newell moved from his farm in Cardiff — and away from his angry neighbors — and bought another near Syracuse. Henry Martin threatened to "humbug the American people within two years, and [make] the Cardiff giant [seem like] a wooden nutmeg affair." Nothing ever came of this threat and Martin disappeared from the public view. Edward Burkhardt was never paid a penny beyond what Hull gave him to excavate, haul, and arrange to have the gypsum block carved. He later claimed to have designed and carved the statue himself, but he never did anything else regarding the scheme.

Because fraud was never proved before the January deadline, Hull sued the remaining owners for monies owed him. And won. The owners who had managed to sell their shares early on escaped the lawsuit and got to keep whatever profits they had made. Those who came late to the game were stuck with the bill. One of the last to buy into the giant was Stephen Thorne, who had mortgaged his farm to buy his share of the giant, but had no money to pay Hull. Even though the court relieved him of a portion of the debt, he was ruined financially.

Another owner, Amos Westcott, was able to pay Hull what he owed him and came away in decent financial shape. But the embarrassment about being a part of a national fraud (and for having defended it so publicly) haunted Westcott. In July 1873, Westcott locked himself in his bedroom and shot himself, dying before medical help could reach him.

According to *The Giantmaker*, Hull made between $15,000 ($244,000) and $20,000 ($325,000), a good deal of money, but not the fortune he had anticipated. And he never really undermined the religious beliefs of many people. His only recourse was to have the book produced, in which he took the lion's share of the credit for thinking up and carrying out what he saw as a clever practical joke.

Of course, nothing Hull did was ever straightforward. His original partner in the book project, Ezra Walrath, began researching and writing the book. But along the way Hull decided to let John Rankin oversee the making of the book — and never bothered to tell Walrath. Rankin and Hull then contracted with Samuel Crocker to do the actual writing.

Walrath sent Hull a finished manuscript, but Hull avoided paying him anything by claiming that publishers simply weren't interested in the story. Hull then shared the text with Crocker, who may have used parts of it in his own version. Crocker delivered his text, but Hull put it aside to work on another elaborate and time-consuming scheme he hoped would make him rich and famous.

This hoax was much like the Cardiff Giant and had Hull and a partner creating a creature that was the "missing link" between apes and humans. It was made from portland cement, stood seven and a half feet tall, weighed over six hundred pounds, and sported a four-inch-long tail.

Hull and his partner ran out of money before he could bury his new giant, so Hull turned to his onetime giant rival, P. T. Barnum, for cash. It took Hull almost ten years, but eventually the new giant was buried and "discovered" in

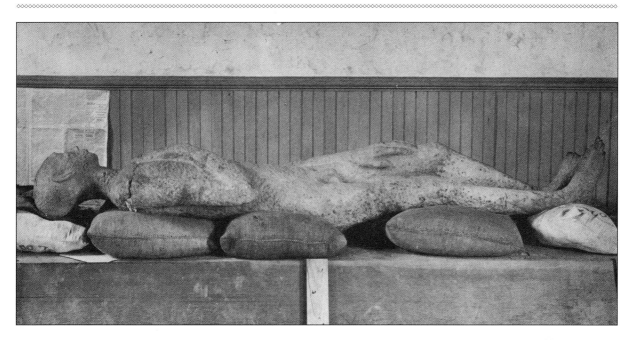

The Colorado Giant resting comfortably on pillows.

Colorado, and it did attract a good deal of attention at first. But the sour feelings left by the Cardiff Giant episode came back to bite Hull. Scientists refused to become involved with the Colorado Giant, and newspapers tended to ridicule the discovery. The *Syracuse Daily Journal* commented sarcastically, "We have always felt confident that the Cardiff Giant had relatives somewhere. . . ." It took only two months for the Colorado Giant to fizzle out and pass into humbug history.

By this time, Hull was broke and being hounded by creditors. To make money, Hull began turning in illegal fishermen at a private lake for a meager bounty of $12.50 apiece. His last hope for big money was the book project. Over the years, first Walrath, and then Crocker, had died, so Hull gave all the book material he had to Rankin, who then began assembling the final version of the story that would become *The Giantmaker.*

Before the text could be sold to a publisher, fate stepped in to end Hull's career as a smooth-talking, deal-making fraud artist. He died in October 1902, at eighty-one years of age (and thirty-

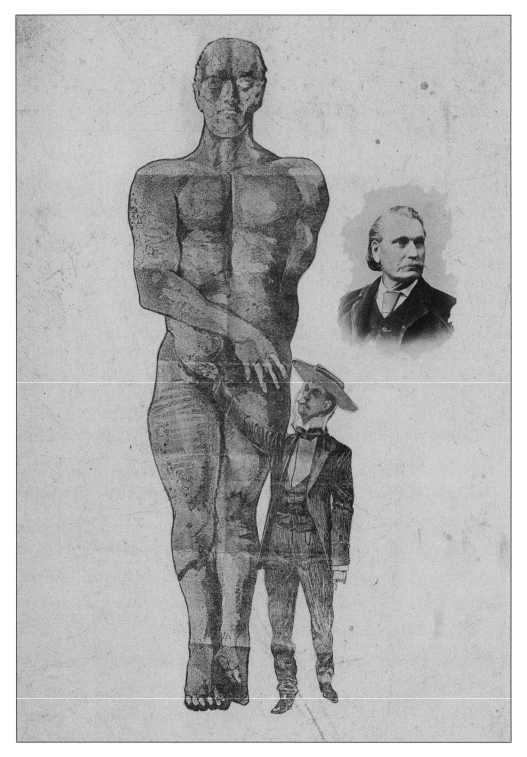

An illustration created for The Giantmaker *that was found in John Rankin's personal papers.*

three years after the Cardiff Giant's miraculous discovery). Rankin submitted the manuscript to various publishers, but each felt the book whitewashed Hull's financial deception, and the book was never published.

To his dying day, Hull never seemed bothered by the way he had taken money from people under false pretenses, that some people suffered great financial losses, or that one person had killed himself over the aftermath of the scheme. Hull's only regret: "I made many mistakes in the management of my scheme or today I would have been a rich man."

Feelings about the Cardiff Giant and Hull have varied over the years. All those who were a part of Hull's scheme — whether they were partners, hired hands, or, like Walrath, were promised financial reward — viewed him as little better than a common criminal. This was especially true of the people who had invested in the giant late in the game and never recovered their money. With the sad exception of Westcott, few expressed regret over their part in the hoax or that they had duped newspapermen, scientists, and tens of thousands of people. They viewed the giant as a business deal and felt Hull had not lived up to his side of the bargain.

A few newspapers seemed willing to view Hull's scheme as clever. In 1871, the *New York Daily Tribune* praised him: "The world must confess that it was never humbugged so brilliantly as it was a year ago last summer by the discovery of the petrified man near Syracuse, N.Y. The Cardiff Giant was the work of no ordinary genius."

Most other newspapers continued to hold a harder view of the whole affair. Ten years after the hoax, the *Cleveland Daily Herald* condemned everyone involved with the Cardiff Giant: "As I contemplated [what is called] the most gigantic humbug of the 19th century, I felt I could proscribe no limitations to American ingenuity in the pursuit of filthy lucre."

In fact, newspapers began to reflect what more and more Americans were feeling about the social and economic changes taking place around them. The Industrial Revolution created a modern

As the United States turned more and more into an industrial giant, large factories began to appear across the country.

urban-industrial economy, plus a national transportation and communications network. The individuals who financed and controlled the factories, railroads, steamship lines, telegraph companies, and banks grew fabulously wealthy, in part because they paid low wages to workers, provided them with no benefits, and allowed unsafe working conditions to exist.

The era (which came to be called the Gilded Age) was also notorious for its unchecked greed, the ostentatious display of wealth by the rich, and political corruption. Ordinary people hungered for a simpler, less commercial, and what they saw as a more honest time, and began to criticize anyone who seemed avaricious or underhanded. Because the Cardiff Giant had captivated and ultimately disappointed such a huge number of Americans, it became an easy target for this anger. Andrew White summarized his feelings about Hull and the others involved in the hoax with, "The Cardiff Giant brought out the worst in these folks, demonstrated the unbridled self-interest and individualism that represented the excesses of [American] democracy."

But this anger at the excesses of the Gilded Age and public hoaxes did have some positive results: By exposing how Americans had been exploited, author Scott Tribble said, incidents like the Cardiff Giant actually "pointed the way to reform. . . . This new generation of reformers emerged from the increasingly modern American university, targeting corrupt city bosses, noncompetitive business practices, as well as exploitation of labor."

The latter part of the nineteenth century saw reformers establish a number of organizations aimed at increasing professional standards, such as the American Historical Association and the American Medical Association. Most of these orga-

nizations took on the responsibility of monitoring and disciplining members who violated their codes of ethics. Graduate programs were set up in a number of universities to better train journalists, archaeologists, anthropologists, geologists, and students in a number of other sciences. And the Smithsonian's Bureau of American Ethnology began anthropologic research, helping to expose and correct a number of frauds and myths in American history.

These experts and their accumulated knowledge made pulling another Cardiff Giant hoax less likely. Instead of rushing to announce an opinion on a new discovery, experts grew cautious, aware that their professional reputations were at stake. And possibly their jobs. It became customary to bring in other experts to examine and test a find before an opinion was offered.

In addition, experts realized that they often had to argue against public opinion when stating their findings. Andrew White understood how the popularity of an opinion could be extremely daunting. It was, he noted, a "peculiarly

American superstition that the correctness of a belief is decided by the number of people who can be induced to adopt it." So instead of immediately publishing and debating their opinions in the daily newspapers, experts began submitting them in detailed written form to professional journals, where other experts could study and debate their contents. Such care reduced the chances that a fraud similar to the Cardiff Giant could happen again — but didn't eliminate it altogether.

At least twelve imitations of the Cardiff Giant were discovered after it had been proven a fake, including Hull's own Colorado Man. The shelf life of these fakes all turned out to be surprisingly brief, stirring up public interest via the newspapers for a week or two, but quickly being dismissed by experts. And at least one petrified baby was found in 1875 in the gravel bank of the Pine River in Michigan. Local curiosity was stirred, but this fraud was soon condemned as a "second edition of the Cardiff Giant."

The negative opinion about the Cardiff Giant lingered into the twenti-

Once the hoax was revealed, the Cardiff Giant appeared in county fairs for what amounted to pocket change.

eth century. In 1907, then-president Theodore Roosevelt grew impatient with writers he considered "nature fakers," people who romanticized the wilderness in what he saw as a silly and false way. In an article for *Everybody's Magazine*, the president took such well-known writers as Ernest Thompson Seton, William J. Long, and Jack London to task, saying, "There is now no more excuse for being deceived by their stories than for being still in doubt about the silly Cardiff hoax."

As for the Cardiff Giant himself, he was moving here and there, changing hands at least eight times between 1910 and 1935, with his price dropping as low as $100. In 1935, the publisher of the *Des Moines Register and Tribune*, Gardner Cowles Jr., bought the giant and put him on display in his knotty-pine basement (which he called his "whoopee room"), complete with several old posters from the giant's original tour.

By this time, all of the main players in the Cardiff Giant hoax were long

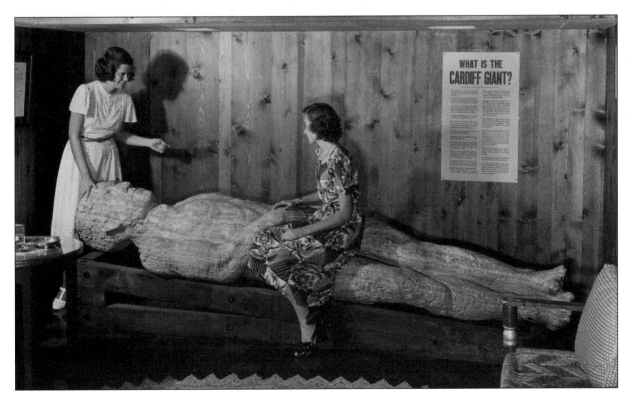

The Cardiff Giant resting comfortably in Gardner Cowles's knotty-pine basement.

A mock funeral was held at the Farmers' Museum in 1948 for their newest guest.

dead and memories had faded about the financial and personal tragedies it had caused. People began to view it as a symbol from a more innocent and naive past, a silly and humorous episode and little more. Carl Carmer turned this emerging myth into "history" in his 1936 book of American folklore, *Listen for a Lonesome Drum*. It was all a big joke, Carmer insisted: "The whole country bent just about double over Stub Newell's giant and how he fooled the professors — and six million people went to look at him."

Finally, in 1948, the Farmers' Museum acquired the Cardiff Giant from Cowles and installed the stone giant in its museum in Cooperstown, New York. On the day the exhibit opened, the museum staged a mock funeral, which featured the giant lying in a large, open grave. The facility's librarian at the time, James Taylor Dunn, seemed to have forgotten or excused the darker aspects of the prank when he welcomed the giant with these words: "It is appropriate that this American belly laugh in stone, the greatest sensation ever known on a New York

A duplicate Cardiff Giant appears in Marvin's Marvelous Mechanical Museum in Farmington Hills, Michigan.

State farm, should end its days at the Farmers' Museum, which seeks ... to portray every aspect of life in this state."

One would think that the real Cardiff Giant could at last rest in peace for eternity as a major museum attraction. But no, competition has surfaced once again, this time in Farmington Hills, Michigan. Standing eleven feet tall, what is billed as "The Cardiff Giant" looms over the arcade machines, sideshow wonders, and coin-operated fortune-tellers at Marvin's Marvelous Mechanical Museum. The explanation sign for Marvin's colossus does mention (in very small type) that this stone giant is actually the one P. T. Barnum had made for his museum. So even in retirement the original Cardiff Giant has stiff competition for the public's attention.

And so George Hull (with his Cardiff Giant) comes down to us today, linked with P. T. Barnum (and his Feejee Mermaid) and Colonel Joseph Wood (and the Great Zeuglodon) as benign individuals who committed nothing more than elaborate practical jokes. There are indeed humorous aspects to these and other such hoax stories, but there are also cautions. It's important to remember that at the heart of each episode, whether done for profit or laughs, was deception.

The team of experts at the esteemed National Geographic Society certainly wish they had remembered this lesson back in 1999.

In October of that year, the society held a major press conference at their headquarters to announce a significant fossil find. It was called *Archaeoraptor liaoningensis*, a chicken-size dinosaur that presumably lived from 125 million to 140 million years ago. At the same time, an article appeared in *National Geographic* magazine in which author Christopher P. Sloan noted that the fossil's "long arms and small body scream 'Bird!' It's long, stiff tail . . . screams 'Dinosaur!'" It was, Sloan announced, "a true missing link in the complex chain that connects dinosaurs to birds."

Only it wasn't. It seems that a Chinese farmer had found two separate fossils and glued them together, hoping to sell it for a handsome price to visiting fossil hunters. It eventually ended up at the National Geographic Society and in the excitement over discovering this "missing link," their paleontologists overlooked obvious warning signs. They even ignored doubts raised by the Smithsonian Institution's Curator of Birds Storrs Olson, who pointed out specific problems he saw in the fossil and asked that other experts be brought in to examine it. In the rush to be the first to

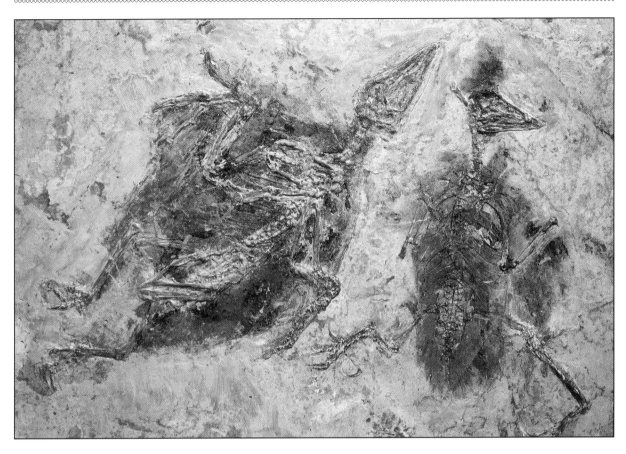

In a much publicized press conference, the National Geographic Society proudly displayed Archaeoraptor liaoningensis *as the missing link between dinosaurs and birds.*

publish the story, *National Geographic* didn't bother to bring in any other experts.

When the hoax was revealed, a frustrated and angry Olson exploded, "National Geographic has reached an all-time low for engaging in sensationalistic, unsubstantiated, tabloid journalism." A highly embarrassed National Geographic Society apologized for its blunder and tried to explain how it had been fooled. And its exasperated editor in chief, William Allen, wondered, "How did we get into this mess?"

The answer, of course, is the same one that anyone who has been duped by a similar scam might answer: What they saw looked authentic enough even to their expert eyes. But in the end, they saw *exactly* what they wanted to see.

Other Famous Hoaxes

The Cardiff Giant was an archaeological hoax (that is, the stone giant was supposed to have been the product of an ancient society). There have been many archaeological hoaxes, some done for money, some for religious reasons or advancement in a profession, and some simply as a practical joke. Here is a brief list of some notable frauds.

Johann Beringer was the dean of medicine at the University of Wurzburg in 1725, but he fancied himself a rather good amateur archaeologist as well. One day while searching for fossils on a nearby mountain, he came across some very unusual rocks. The rocks were all carved with the shapes of various plants, lizards, frogs, and spiders on their webs, along with shooting stars and planets, and accompanied with Greek and Hebrew letters.

Beringer was beside himself with joy, believing he had found physical proof that God had created the earth and that "God, the Father of Nature, would fill our minds with His praises and perfections radiating from these wondrous effects." The truth was

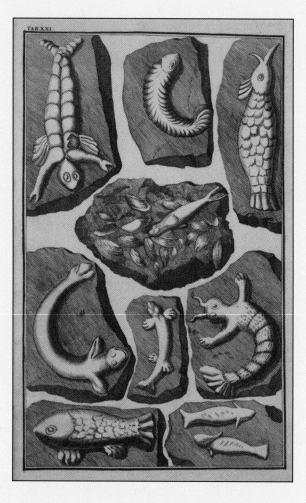

Johann Beringer thought he had discovered ancient stones that proved that God had created the earth.

that the stones had been manufactured by the school's geography professor and a librarian, who both believed that Beringer was a pompous windbag who needed to be taught a lesson.

The two pranksters realized they had gone too far when Beringer announced he was planning to publish a book describing the meaning of his remarkable find. They confessed what they had done, but Beringer refused to believe them and had his book published anyway. Months later, Beringer realized that he had in fact been duped, but it was too late. His reputation was forever tarnished. As for the two who carried out the scheme, one was fired from his job, while the other was demoted and denied access to the library he had once run.

In 1860, archaeologist **David Wyrick** was digging through Native American burial grounds near Newark, Ohio, when he came across what have come to be called the Newark Holy Stones. Each stone had Hebrew inscribed in them, and Wyrick was convinced they proved that nonnative people had visited the area hundreds, if not thousands, of years before Columbus.

Wyrick wrote a book about the Newark Holy Stones, complete with woodcuts of the sacred objects. But even before publication of his book, experts were ridiculing them as frauds, pointing to the many spelling

David Wyrick claimed that his discovery of the Newark Holy Stones showed that people from Europe had visited America thousands of years before Columbus. This one, known as "The Decalogue," shows Moses in a long robe with a shortened version of the Ten Commandments carved around the border.

errors. Some people suspect that Wyrick perpetrated the fraud to enhance his career. Others believe a local Episcopal minister planted them, hoping to convince the world that Adam and Eve were the parents to all races and to suggest that all people were indeed created equal.

Charles Dawson was an amateur archaeologist who very desperately wanted to be taken seriously by real archaeologists, especially those who were members of the prestigious British Royal Academy. It was then his good fortune in 1912 to discover fossilized bone fragments in a gravel pit in

Charles Dawson discussing his Piltdown Man with a group of learned scientists. It would take decades for his discovery to be exposed as a fraud.

Piltdown, a village in East Sussex, England. Dawson immediately took the fragments to the keeper of geology at London's Natural History Museum, Sir Arthur Smith Woodward.

Woodward was impressed and soon joined Dawson at Piltdown to help uncover even more pieces of a skull and jawbone. Other scientists began studying the fossils and came to the conclusion that they were from an ancient ancestor of humans some 500,000 years old. Eager scientists named the creature *Eoanthropus dawsoni* (Dawson's Dawn Man) and declared him "the earliest specimen of true humanity yet discovered."

There were a few doubters, of course. The Smithsonian Institution's Gerrit S. Miller came to the conclusion that if the jawbone and cranium were actually combined, it would create a freakish creature never found in real life. He was shouted down by colleagues, and so what came to be known as the Piltdown Man was considered a genuine link to our past and studied seriously for over forty years.

It took Joseph Weiner, a professor of physical anthropology at Oxford University, to unearth the fraud in 1950. It turned out that these "ancient" fossils were actually a medieval man's skull, a five-hundred-year-old orangutan jaw, and the teeth of a chimpanzee, all cleverly pieced together. It was, in Weiner's words, "a most elaborate and carefully prepared hoax . . . so unscrupulous and inexplicable, as to find no parallel in paleontological history." Dawson died in 1916, firmly believing that his name would go down in history as the discoverer of the missing link between apes and humans; instead his hoax is remembered as "an ugly trick played by a warped and unscrupulous mind."

Shinichi Fujimura appeared to have a blessed career as a leading amateur archaeologist, taking part in over 180 digs in northern Japan. He almost always found important artifacts, their age becoming increasingly older. His finds extended the Japanese Paleolithic period from approximately 30,000 years to about 300,000 years BC.

There were doubters, including Shizuo Oda and Charles T. Keally, who wrote that "no proven artifacts of human origin predating 30,000 BC" exist. Eyebrows were

Shinichi Fujimura talking to reporters about another of his remarkable finds.

raised by this and other similar claims, but Fujimura was so famous and revered in the field that the doubters were easily dismissed as jealous rivals.

Then, on October 23, 2000, Fujimura and his team announced another startling discovery, a find that pushed human settlements in northern Japan back to 570,000 years BC. The field of archaeology was once again abuzz with praise for Fujimura — until a series of photographs appeared in the *Mainichi Shimbun* newspaper. They show Fujimura digging holes and planting arti-facts one day before his team dug them up. Fujimura confessed to the deception, explaining that he was "possessed by an uncontrollable urge" and that the things he planted were from his own collection. He knew that no accurate way existed to test the age of the items he planted and guessed that placing them in very ancient strata would suggest they were themselves very ancient. Fujimura, who was said to have had "divine hands" because of his astonishing success rate, has since retired entirely from the business of digging up ancient artifacts.

A Word About My Research

In the fall of 2008, Bernie Madoff, a renowned and esteemed financier and former president of the New York Stock Exchange, was arrested for the biggest Ponzi scheme in financial history. Over the course of many years, he had managed to bilk investors in his financial management business out of between 18 and 68 billion (yes, billion) dollars. Most of these investors had no idea that he was taking in and using their money and not investing it as he claimed. Instead, he created false accounting records to cover up what he was really doing. Like many people, I was appalled and fascinated by the monumental size of Madoff's theft and even considered writing a book about it, but hesitated. While a "ripped from the headlines" sort of story would be immediate and might grab people's attention, I knew that all of the facts (such as who exactly knew about his scheme and why some obvious warning signs were ignored by regulatory officials) would take years to unearth and interpret. Even a thoughtfully done instant book would lack historical perspective and be more of a glorified magazine piece (and might well be out-of-date pretty quickly) than a book that might be accurate for years.

Then I thought I might write about Charles Ponzi and the scheme he cooked up in 1919 that netted him over 2 million dollars and linked his name forever with other such "Ponzi" schemes. But here's where two additional problems became clear. I did not find either Madoff or Ponzi very interesting people — they were/are dull little men — and writing about financial dealings lacks drama and action.

Which was when I remembered the Cardiff Giant. Financially, it was small potatoes when compared to what Ponzi and Madoff did, but the fact that the giant was so convincing to so many people, even the supposed experts, was amazing and instructive, and the large cast of characters includes some truly unusual and eccentric folk.

I began doing research just as winter was setting in and decided to put off visiting the scene of the event in New York State until warmer spring weather returned. So I spent the winter reading everything I could find about the Cardiff Giant and the people involved. I located many of these books and articles on the Internet and was able to either download them to my computer or purchase them from antique-book sites. Among the sites I used were www.ancestry.com; news.google.com/archivesearch; Google Book Search; newspaperarchive.com; www.bookfinder.com; and xooleanswers.com. By the time warmer May temperatures arrived, I had not only read a great deal about the incident and the times, but had also begun thinking about how I would write the text. And I was ready to travel.

Traveling to the region where a book's events took place is important and has many benefits. For instance, the only way to read John Rankin's *The Giantmaker* was to visit the Broome County Historical Society in Binghamton, New York, where they have a manuscript copy of it. Stops at other historical societies let me study newspapers from the time in a careful page-by-page way and to discover other treasures such as pamphlets and flyers and photographs. At the New York State Historical Association in Cooperstown, I was able to read Scott Tribble's doctoral thesis about the Cardiff Giant, out of which grew his very informative book, *A Colossal Hoax*. Of course, I went to the Farmers' Museum (just across the street from the Historical Association) to see the Cardiff Giant up close. He's tucked away in a corner behind a wall covered with pictures and text that tell about his rapid rise to fame and just as rapid fall from favor. He's somewhat worse for wear, but he is impressive and I could imagine what it must have been like for Newell's well-diggers to unearth him.

Naturally, traveling to Onondaga County literally let me see the landscape and buildings (many from the nineteenth century survive) and helped me to conjure up what the area might have been like over one hundred years ago. In the case of Cardiff, New York, it seems that things haven't changed very much. Granted, the roads are paved and there are TV satellite dishes here and there, but the population is about the same as it was in 1869. And while most of the agricultural fields are overgrown with weeds, the contours of the land remain unchanged. This is especially true when you come across the historical marker on Tully Farms Road just across from where Newell's farm once was.

If you close your eyes, you can almost hear the clomp of horses' hooves and the creaking of wagon wheels that greeted Stub Newell in the days after his great discovery.

I could not have done this research without the generous, thoughtful help of many experts. I especially want to thank Sarah Kozma of the Onondaga Historical Association Museum and Research Center; Gerald Smith of the Broome County Historical Society; Erin Richardson, Director of Collections, New York State Historical Association; Anne Smith, Town of Lafayette historian; L. Jane Tracy, Town of Onondaga historian; and Lynn M. Fisher, Town of Tully historian. If I managed to bring alive this odd, intriguing incident from our country's past, it is due to these dedicated and knowledgeable people's direction.

Source Notes

I: The Discovery

Details about the arrival of Gideon Emmons and Henry Nichols at Stub Newell's farm, the general terrain, the digging of the well, and the discovery of the giant come from *Syracuse Daily Standard*, October 18 and 30, 1869.

Information about Emmons's wartime injury was from the *Marathon Mirror*, May 13, 1865.

A very nice discussion of the Onondaga Stone Giants can be found in Anthony Wayne Wonderley, *At the Font of Marvelous: Exploring Oral Narrative and Mythic Imagery of the Iroquois and Their Neighbors* (Syracuse, NY: Syracuse University Press, 2009), pp. 98–104.

Newell's fear that a murder may have been committed is from *Syracuse Daily Journal*, October 20, 1869.

"I declare . . ." Anonymous, *The American Goliah*, p. 3.

"They have found . . ." Anonymous, *The Cardiff Giant Humbug*, p. 26.

"It is a foot . . ." Anonymous, *The Cardiff Giant Humbug*, p. 26.

II: Word Spreads

Details about the first visitors to Newell's farm, Billy Houghton's theory that they had found a petrified human, and the first offers to purchase the discovery were from *Syracuse Daily Journal*, October 18 and 20, 1869; Rankin, *The Giantmaker*, pp. 125–129; and Anonymous, *The Cardiff Giant Humbug*, p. 26.

Information about marine and plant fossils in northwestern New York came from the Rochester Academy of Science: http://www.rasny.org/fossil/NYGeoHistory.htm, and the New York Paleontological Society.

Information about Joshua V. Clark and his quote are from Joshua V. H. Clark, *Onondaga, or Reminiscences of Earlier and Later Times* (Syracuse, NY: Stoddard and Babcock, 1849), Vol. 2, pp. 266–268.

Giants appear in numerous books of the Bible, including Genesis 6:4–5, Numbers 13:28–33, Deuteronomy 2:10, Joshua 12:4, and 1 Samuel 17:4.

Here and throughout to determine the value of an 1869 dollar in today's money, I used MeasuringWorth.com, a website that was founded by Lawrence H. Officer, Professor of Economics at the University of Illinois, Chicago. It can be found at: http://www.measuringworth.com/ppowerus/result.php.

III: The Scientists' Opinions

How John Clark and Silas Forbes helped spread news about the discovery and about the arrival of visitors to Newell's farm on Sunday can be found in *Syracuse Daily Journal*, October 18 and 20, 1869.

A description of the examination of the giant by the four local doctors comes from Rankin, *The Giantmaker*, p. 136.

The first mention of the use of fig leaves for modesty appear in the Bible, Genesis 3:7, after Adam and Eve had eaten the forbidden fruit. "Then the eyes of both were opened, and they knew that they were naked; and they sewed fig leaves together and made themselves aprons." For the most part, however, Greek and Roman artists did not use a fig leaf when depicting the human body, and neither did most European artists until the mid-1500s. That was when Catholic and Protestant church leaders spoke out against the "sinfulness of the flesh," and many masterpieces of art, including works by Raphael, Rubens, Titian, da Vinci, and Michelangelo, were redone to include fig leaves. This tradition continued well into the twentieth century.

John Boynton's life and achievements are detailed in *Syracuse Daily Standard*, October 18, 1869, and *Syracuse Daily Journal*, October 21, 1890. His examination of the stone giant is described in Rankin, *The Giantmaker*, pp. 142–143.

"The chief topic of conversation . . ." *Syracuse Daily Standard*, October 18, 1869.

"For modesty's sake, an improvised 'fig leaf' was kept over the loins . . ." *Syracuse Daily Standard*, October 20, 1869.

IV: Open for Business

The establishment of Newell's new business on Monday, accompanied by the arrival of large crowds, is described in *Syracuse Daily Journal*, *Syracuse Daily Courier*, and *Syracuse Daily Standard*, October 18, 1869.

Details about Billy Houghton's show come from Rankin, *The Giantmaker*, pp. 148–149, and *Syracuse Daily Courier*, October 20, 1869.

Information about Civil War casualties comes from James M. McPherson, *Battle Cry of Freedom: The Civil War Era*, New York, 1988 Oxford University Press, p. 854. Details about Jay Gould, James Fisk, and Andrew Johnson's troubled administration were found in John A Garraty, ed, *The Young Reader's Companion to American History* (Boston: Houghton Mifflin Company, 1994), pp. 456–457, 840, 842.

Newell's various secret business dealings are from Rankin, *The Giantmaker*, pp. 149–161.

"An air of great solemnity . . ." White, *Autobiography of Andrew Dickson White*, Vol. 2, p. 469.

"A man stands at the mouth of the excavation . . ." *Syracuse Daily Courier*, October 20, 1869.

"jest one feller's opinion" *Syracuse Daily Courier*, October 20, 1869.

"The marrow of his bones . . ." White, *Autobiography of Andrew Dickson White*, Vol. 2, p. 472.

"Nothing in the world . . ." White, *Autobiography of Andrew Dickson White*, Vol. 2, p. 472.

"A kindly benevolent smile . . ." *New England Homestead*, October 30, 1869.

"A NEW WONDER . . ." *Syracuse Daily Standard*, October 18, 1869.

"IMPORTANT DISCOVERY . . ." *Syracuse Daily Courier*, October 18, 1869.

"Compared with the Cardiff . . ." *New York Commercial Advertiser*, November 5, 1869.

"extremely unpleasant, uncomfortable [wet] weather" *Syracuse Journal*, October 22, 1869.

"The roads . . . crowded with buggies . . ." White, *Autobiography of Andrew Dickson White*, Vol. 2, p. 469.

V: Changes

Information about the sale of part ownerships in the Cardiff Giant was found in: Rankin, *The Giantmaker*, pp. 149–165; Tribble, *A Colossal Hoax*, pp. 80–84; and *Syracuse Daily Journal*, July 7, 1873.

One member of the group that bought part ownership in the giant was David Hannum, one of the largest land-owners in the area, a shrewd businessman, and a very successful and not always honest horse trader. Even so, Hannum was a charmer, as one biographer noted, "His good nature, however, always stood him in good stead, and many a time the loser went away feeling satisfied just because of Hannum's amusing personality." For more on Hannum, see Vance, *The Real David Harum*, pp. 21–23. Incidentally, P. T. Barnum is usually credited with first saying "There's a sucker born every minute," though most historians now believe Hannum was the first to utter it. See: http://www.historybuff.com/library/refbarnum.html.

Joseph H. Wood, P. T. Barnum, and many other individuals set up private natural history museums in the nineteenth century. Most of these were a strange combination of real and interesting objects, fabricated creatures based on myths and rumors, and various freaks of nature, both human and animal. Interesting books on this phenomenon are Bondeson, *The Fejee Mermaid and Other Essays in Natural and Unnatural History*; Dennett, *Weird and Wonderful*; and Thompson, *The Mystery and Lore of Monsters*.

Descriptions of the new show organized by Colonel Joseph H. Wood were from *Syracuse Daily Standard*, *Syracuse Daily Courier*, and *Syracuse Daily Journal*, October 25, 1869.

"Sunday was a crusher . . ." *Syracuse Daily Standard*, October 25, 1869.

"were compelled . . ." *Syracuse Daily Courier*, October 25, 1869.

"The proprietors of the . . ." *Syracuse Daily Courier*, November 2, 1869.

"It is the opinion of Mr. Owen . . ." *Rochester Democrat*, October 20, 1869.

"Will anyone say . . ." *Syracuse Daily Standard*, November 1, 1869.

"Is it not strange . . ." White, *Autobiography of Andrew Dickson White*, Vol. 2, p. 472.

"It is positively absurd . . ." *Syracuse Daily Standard*, October 21, 1869.

"May not a wandering sculptor . . ." *Syracuse Daily Journal*, November 2, 1869.

"The Giant . . . is a statue . . ." *Syracuse Daily Journal*, October 26, 1869.

"The statue, being colossal . . ." *Syracuse Daily Standard*, October 21, 1869.

"Altogether, it is the most remarkable . . ." *Syracuse Daily Journal*, October 26, 1869.

"The Syracuse people . . ." *New York Commercial Advertiser*, October 21, 1869.

VI: Embarrassing Accusations

Rumors that the statue might be a fraud began almost immediately as stated in *Syracuse Daily Journal*, October 19, 1869. Also see Rankin, *The Giantmaker*, pp. 183–187.

Information about George Hull was found in Anonymous, *The Cardiff Giant Humbug*; Rankin, *The Giantmaker*; and Tribble, *A Colossal Hoax*.

Discussions about how often hoaxes were perpetrated in western New York State were found in *The Knickerbocker* 46, no. 5 (November 1855), p. 532; *Syracuse Daily Standard*, October 18, 1869; *New York Herald*, October 21 and 25, 1869.

The Thomas B. Ellis letter that spoke about Jules Geraud and his statue appeared in *New York Herald*, October 25, 1869.

"Why, all this show and parade . . ." *Syracuse Daily Standard*, November 2, 1869.

"Those eyes looked right at us . . ." Tribble, *A Colossal Hoax*, p. 33.

"The grossest, foulest . . ." Ezra Champion Seaman, *The American System of Government* (New York: Charles Scribner & Co., 1870), p. 53.

"Western New York . . ." *New York Herald*, October 25, 1869.

"A STUPENDOUS HOAX . . ." *New York Herald*, October 25, 1869.

"It has the marks of the ages . . ." Anonymous, *The American Goliah*, p. 30.

"His good character . . ." *Syracuse Daily Journal*, October 28, 1869.

"Lacking greatly in the upper story . . ." *Syracuse Daily Standard*, October 30, 1869.

"As I have looked upon this wonderful object . . ." *Syracuse Daily Courier*, October 20, 1869.

"Joy in believing . . ." White, *Autobiography of Andrew Dickson White*, Vol. 2, p. 466.

VII: The Ugly Truth

Details about the creation of the Cardiff Giant, its transportation, and its burial were found in Rankin, *The Giantmaker*; *The History of Sauk County, Wisconsin* (Chicago: Western Historical Co., 1880), pp. 549–550; Anonymous, *The Cardiff Giant Humbug*, pp. 16–17, 19, 20–21, 23, 32; "The History of the Cardiff Giant Hoax," *New Englander and Yale Review* 34, no. 133 (October 1875), p. 764; *Syracuse Daily Journal*, January 29, 1870.

Details about the Feejee Mermaid were located in Barnum, *The Life of P. T. Barnum, Written by Himself*, pp. xvii–xviii and 214–245; and Bondeson, *The Feejee Mermaid and Other Essays on Natural and Unnatural History*, pp. 36–63.

The primitive state of archaeology, geology, paleontology, and other sciences in the United States was found in Tribble, *A Colossal Hoax*, pp. xi, 19–20, 24–25, 105–106, and 193.

"We live in the midst . . ." The Reverend Benjamin Martin's remarks were made in "Science and the Scriptures," a discourse before the New-York Alpha of the Phi Beta Kappa Society, delivered at Union College, Schenectady, July 27, 1852.

"Americans . . . were easy targets . . ." Kasson, John F., *Civilizing the Machine: Technology and Republican Values in America, 1776–1900*, p. xii–xiv.

"Geologists say it was at one time a lake . . ." "He made the Giant," *The Reading Eagle*, Sunday, February 10, 1889, p. 2.

VIII: A Giant Move

The removal of the Cardiff Giant from Newell's farm and his installation in Syracuse are detailed in *Syracuse Daily Journal* and *Syracuse Daily Courier*, November 6, 1869; and *Syracuse Daily Standard*, November 6 and 8, 1869. Also see Rankin, *The Giantmaker*, pp. 235–236.

The poem "Take Him Up Gently" comes from *Syracuse Daily Courier*, November 6, 1869.

Information about the Industrial Revolution and its effect on rural communities was found in Garraty, *The Young Reader's Companion to American History*, pp. 144, 375–376, 432–433, and 654–655, as well as from Donald Kagan, Steven Ozment, and Frank M. Turner, *The Western Heritage* (Upper Saddle River, NJ: Pearson, Prentice Hall, 2004), pp. 453, 744–746, 750–752, and 756–759.

Crowd estimates were found in *Syracuse Daily Journal*, November 9, 14, and 15, 1869; and *Syracuse Daily Standard*, November 12 and 13, 1869.

The contract for sale of part interest in the giant to John Rankin was found in John C. Rankin papers, 1857–1963, 1869–1902, Broome County Historical Society, Broome County Public Library, Binghamton, NY.

"For the present . . ." *Syracuse Daily Journal*, November 4, 1869.

"The future having failed them . . ." Kasson, *Civilizing the Machine*, pp. xii–xiv.

"[The Giant] had the potential . . ." Kasson, *Civilizing the Machine*, pp. 133.

IX: Enter Barnum

Information about P. T. Barnum, how he arranged to acquire his own statue, and how he displayed it in New York was located in the following sources: Barnum, *Funny Stories Told by Phineas T. Barnum*, pp. 332–333; Rankin, *The Giantmaker*, pp. 279, 283–285, 293–297; *A Giant Hoax*, pp. 146–147; *Daily Evening Bulletin*, December 17, 1869; *Syracuse Daily Courier*, December 8, 1869; *Syracuse Daily Journal*, December 4, 1869; *New York Sun*, December 7 and 22, 1869; *New York Commercial Advertiser*, December 7 and 11, 1869; *New York Evening Post*, December 7, 1869; and *New York Tribune*, December 6 and 11, 1869.

More can be found on how the owners of the original Cardiff Giant reacted to Barnum's imitation, and the subsequent lawsuit in Rankin, *The Giantmaker*, p. 319; *Albany Evening Journal*, December 7, 1869; *New York Sun*, December 22, 1869; *New York Tribune*, December 13 and 14, 1869; and *Syracuse Daily Courier*, December 17, 1869.

Information about the giant face-off and how Barnum triumphed was found in *New York Commercial Advertiser*, December 18, 1869; *New York Sun*, December 22, 1869; *Syracuse Daily Standard*, December 29, 1869; and *Syracuse Daily Journal*, December 18, 20, and 21, 1869; January 4, 6, 12, 21, and 29, 1870; and February 5, 1870.

"His stone majesty" Tribble, *A Colossal Hoax*, p. 165.

"imitation of the original" Tribble, pp. 167–168.

"[Carl Franz Otto] was led to make this attempt . . ." *Syracuse Daily Journal*, November 13, 1869.

"A MOST IMPRESSIVE . . ." *New York Daily Tribune*, December 6, 1869.

"We forbear to distinguish . . ." *New York Herald*, December 7, 1869.

"Truth is mighty and must prevail . . ." *New York Commercial Advertiser*, December 11, 1869.

"A plaster cast . . ." *New York Daily Tribune*, December 13, 1869.

"It is rather rich . . ." *Philadelphia Inquirer*, December 14, 1869.

"Two men of gypsum . . ." *New York Commercial Advertiser*, December 18, 1869.

"Barnum has thus . . ." *New York Sun*, December 22, 1869.

X: Giant Problems All Around

Fillmore Smith's letter appeared in *Syracuse Daily Courier*, October 29, 1869.

John Boynton's responses to Smith's letter appeared in *Syracuse Daily Courier* and *Syracuse Daily Journal*, November 17, 1869.

O. C. Marsh's recollections about his investigation of the Cardiff Giant first appeared in *Buffalo Courier*, November 29, 1869; and reprinted in *Syracuse Daily Courier*, November 30, 1869; and in *New York Herald* and *New York Sun*, December 1, 1869.

Ezra Walrath had been an editor at the *Syracuse Daily Courier*, but was in the real estate and loan business when the Cardiff Giant was discovered. He also kept the financial records for Hull's various businesses, so he knew Hull very well. According to Rankin, *The Giantmaker*, pp. 152, 190, 221–222, and 250–251, he joined an anti–Cardiff Giant group composed of the men who had been rejected in their bid to buy the giant, and later accepted Hull's offer to write a book about the hoax.

Information about the rush of the owners to sell their shares of the Cardiff Giant was found in Tribble, *A Colossal Hoax*, pp. 196–198.

Details about Carl Otto's other imitation giants were located in *Syracuse Daily Journal*, December 18, 20, and 21, 1869; January 4, 6, 12, 21, and 24, 1870; and February 5, 1870.

Information about business law was obtained from informal discussions with Lawrence Solan, and Don Forchelli Professor of Law, Brooklyn Law School.

Details about the various Cardiff Giant imitations were located in Tribble, *A Colossal Hoax*, pp. 221–222.

"Now let me ask . . ." *Syracuse Daily Standard*, October 30, 1869.

"The Doctor frankly confessed . . ." *Syracuse Daily Standard*, November 23, 1869.

"Dr. Boynton [is] not a high authority . . ." This quote was originally published in the *Worcester Spy* and reprinted in *Syracuse Daily Courier*, November 24, 1869.

"I believe the Cardiff Giant is made of that great block of gypsum . . ." *The Cardiff Giant Humbug*, p. 30.

"A certain person . . ." *Syracuse Daily Courier*, December 1, 1869.

XI: A Giant Farewell

Information about the Cardiff Giant's trip to Boston and its examination by Ralph Waldo Emerson and other notable individuals was located in Rankin, *The Giantmaker*, pp. 326–329; *Boston Morning Journal*, January 25 and 26, 1870; *Boston Daily Evening Transcript*, January 27, 1870; and *Boston Post*, January 26 and February 7, 1870.

Gott's purchase of the giant and its subsequent wanderings were found in *Lowell Daily Citizen and News*, May 23 and 31, and June 3, 1870; *Syracuse Daily Journal*, July 20, 1870, December 5, 1870, June 3, 1871, and July 19, 1871; *Utica Press*, September 20, 1924; *New York Daily Tribune*, September 21, 1871; *Syracuse Herald*, August 5, 1913; and in a clipping entitled "Cardiff Giant Now Stored in a Barn," New-York Historical Society, 1913.

"A big thing . . ." *Boston Post*, January 24, 1870.

"With a microscope . . ." Rankin, *The Giantmaker*, pp. 326–329.

"Our readers are familiar . . ." *Boston Morning Journal*, January 25, 1870.

"We now have ample proof . . ." *Syracuse Daily Journal*, January 24, 1870.

"The behavior of Hull . . ." *New York Daily Tribune*, reprinted in *The Christian Union*, March 27, 1870.

"vulgar fraud . . ." *Albany Evening Journal*, December 15, 1869.

"And who is not tired . . ." *Syracuse Daily Journal*, February 8, 1870.

XII: A Final Resting Place

What happened to the various people involved in creating and exhibiting the Cardiff Giant is nicely summarized in Tribble, *A Colossal Hoax*, pp. 189–191, 192, and 196–198.

Stephen Thorne's financial troubles were discussed in *Utica Press*, September 20, 1924.

Westcott's death is noted in *Syracuse Daily Journal*, July 7, 1873.

Information about the writing of *The Giantmaker* was found in Tribble, *A Colossal Hoax*, pp. 191–192 and 228–229.

Details about Hull's Colorado Giant hoax were found in Conant, *History of the Geological Wonder of the World*, pp. 2–8; Tribble, *A Colossal Hoax*, pp. 204, 205–206 and 207–208; *New York Daily Tribune*, October 5, 1877, and January 24, 1878; *New-York Semi-Weekly Tribune*, March 8, 1878; *Daily Rocky Mountain News*, December 16, 1877, and January 27, 1878; *New York Herald*, December 8, 1877; and *New York Times*, December 16, 1877, and January 27, 1878.

A discussion of the Gilded Era and its excesses can be found in Garraty, *The Young Reader's Companion to American History*, pp. 711–712.

More can be learned about the positive changes following the Gilded Age in Tribble, *A Colossal Hoax*, pp. 233–235.

The sale of the giant to Gardner Cowles Jr. is recounted in Gardner Cowles, *Mike Looks Back* (New York: Gardner Cowles, 1985), pp. 56–57.

"It is appropriate that this American belly laugh . . ." You can learn more about the Farmers' Museum at http://www.farmersmuseum.org.

You can see the original Cardiff Giant's only existing rival at http://marvin3m.com.

Details about the National Geographic Society and the 1999 fraud can be found in Christopher Sloan, "Feathers for T. rex?" *National Geographic* 196, no. 5 (November 1999), 98–107; Simons, Lewis M., "A Fossil Trail," *National Geographic* 198, no. 4 (October 2000), pp. 128–132. Storrs Olson's letter about the hoax can be found at http://dml.cmnh.org/1999Nov/msg00263.html.

"We have always felt confident . . ." *Syracuse Daily Journal*, October 2, 1877.

"I made many mistakes . . ." *Galveston Daily News*, January 2, 1878.

"The world must confess . . ." *New York Daily Tribune*, September 21, 1871.

"As I contemplated . . ." *Cleveland Daily Herald*, reprinted in the *Syracuse Daily Journal*, August 12, 1881.

"The Cardiff Giant brought out the worst in these folks . . ." White, *Autobiography of Andrew Dickson White*, p. 476.

"pointed the way to reform . . ." Tribble, *A Colossal Hoax*, pp. 234–235.

"peculiarly American superstition . . ." White, *Autobiography of Andrew Dickson White*, p. 476.

"There is now no more excuse . . ." This quote was found in Theodore Roosevelt, *The Works of Theodore Roosevelt: Presidential Addresses and State Papers* (New York: P. F. Collier & Son, 1910), pp. 1344–1345.

Other Famous Hoaxes

Johann Beringer: Jahn, Melvin. "Beringer, Johann Bartholomaeus Adam," *Dictionary of Scientific Biography* (New York: Charles Scribner's Sons, 1970), Vol. 2, pp. 15–16. Stephani, Dain, "Histories: Johann Beringer and the Fraudulent Fossils," *New Scientist*, no. 25 (December 2009).

Charles Dawson: Russell, Miles. *Piltdown Man: The Secret Life of Charles Dawson* (London: Tempus, 2004).

Shinichi Fujimura: Feder, Kenneth. *Frauds, Myths, and Mysteries: Science and Pseudoscience in Archaeology* (New York: McGraw-Hill Humanities, 2008).

David Wyrick: Marder, William. *Indians in the Americas: The Untold Story* (San Diego, CA: The Book Tree, 2005), p. 48.

Selected Bibliography

The following bibliography contains books, pamphlets, and articles about the Cardiff Giant.

Anonymous. *The American Goliah: A Wonderful Geological Discovery*. Syracuse, NY: Redington & Howe, 1869. An online version is available at: http://www.gutenberg.org/ebooks/6869.

Anonymous. *The Cardiff Giant Humbug: The Complete and Thorough Exposition of the Greatest Deception of the Age*. Fort Dodge, IA: North West Book and Job Printing Establishment, 1870.

Anonymous. *The Onondaga Giant, or the Great Archaeological Discovery*. Syracuse, NY: Nottingham & Tucker, 1869.

Barnum, P. T. *Funny Stories Told by Phineas T. Barnum*. New York: Routledge & Sons, 1890.

Bondeson, Jan. *The Feejee Mermaid and Other Essays in Natural and Unnatural History*. Ithaca, NY: Cornell University Press, 1999.

Boning, Richard A. *The Cardiff Giant*. Baldwin, NY: Dexter & Westbrook, 1972.

Carmer, Carl. *Listen for a Lonesome Drum: A York State Chronicle*. New York: Farrar & Rinehart, Inc., 1936.

Conant, William A. *History of the Geological Wonder of the World: A Petrified Pre-Historic Human Being*. New York: Wynkoop & Hallenbeck, 1877.

Drummond, A. M., and Robert E. Gard. *The Cardiff Giant: A Chapter in the History of Human Folly, 1869–1870*. Ithaca, NY: Cornell University Press, 1949.

Dunn, James T. *The True, Moral and Diverting Tale of the Cardiff Giant or the American Goliath*. Cooperstown, NY: Farmers' Museum, 1954.

Franco, Barbara. *The Cardiff Giant: A Hundred Year Old Hoax*. Cooperstown, NY: New York State Historical Association, 1969.

Kimball, Gwen. *The Cardiff Giant*. New York: Duell, Sloan and Pearce, 1966.

McKinney, W. A. "The History of the Cardiff Giant Hoax." *New Englander and Yale Review* 34, no. 133 (October 1875): 759–769.

Rankin, John. *The Giantmaker or The Mist of Mystery, A True Story*. 137, item 72, John C. Rankin papers, 1857–1963, 1869–1902, Broome County Historical Society, Broome County Public Library, Binghamton, NY.

Sears, Stephen W. "The Giant in the Earth." *American Heritage* 26, no. 5 (August 1975): 94–99.

Stockwell, G. A. "The Cardiff Giant and Other Frauds." *Popular Science Monthly* 74, no. 13 (June 1878): 197–203.

Summers, James L. *The Cardiff Giants*. Philadelphia: Westminster Press, 1964.

Tribble, Scott. *A Colossal Hoax: The Giant From Cardiff That Fooled America*. Lanham, MD: Rowman & Littlefield Publishers, Inc., 2009.

Vance, Arthur T. *The Real David Harum: The Wise Ways and Droll Sayings of One "Dave" Hannum, of Homer, N.Y., the Original of the Hero of Mr. Westcott's Popular Book — How He Made and Lost a Fortune — His Many Deeds of Charity — Amusing Anecdotes about Him*. New York: Baker and Taylor, 1900.

White, Andrew Dickson. *Autobiography of Andrew Dickson White*. New York: Century Co., 1905.

What follows are books, articles, and websites used to gather historical and cultural information for my book.

Anderson, Ann. *Snake Oil, Hustlers and Hambones: The American Medicine Show.* Jefferson, NC: McFarland & Co., 2000.

Barnum, P. T. *The Life of P. T. Barnum, Written by Himself.* Chicago: University of Illinois Press, 2000.

Blinderman, C. *The Piltdown Inquest.* Buffalo, NY: Prometheus Books, 1986.

Bruce, Robert V. *The Launching of Modern American Science, 1846–1876.* New York: Knopf, 1987.

Callow, Alexander B., Jr. *The Tweed Ring.* New York: Oxford University Press, 1966.

Cashman, Sean Dennis. *America in the Gilded Age: From the Death of Lincoln to the Rise of Theodore Roosevelt.* New York: New York University Press, 1984.

Dennett, Andrea Stulman. *Weird and Wonderful: The Dime Museum in America.* New York: New York University Press, 1997.

Farquhar, Michael. *A Treasure of Deception: Liars, Misleaders, Hoodwinkers, and the Extraordinary True Stories of History's Greatest Hoaxes, Fakes, and Frauds.* New York: Penguin Books, 2005.

Feder, Kenneth L. *Frauds, Myths, and Mysteries: Science and Pseudoscience in Archaeology.* 4th ed., Boston: McGraw-Hill, 2002.

Foner, Eric. *Reconstruction: America's Unfinished Revolution, 1863–1877.* New York: Harper & Row, 1989.

Gillette, William. *The Right to Vote: Politics and the Passage of the Fifteenth Amendment.* Baltimore: Johns Hopkins Press, 1969.

Harris, Neil. *Humbug: The Art of P. T. Barnum.* Chicago: The University of Chicago Press, 1973.

Kasson, John. *Civilizing the Machine: Technology and Republican Values in America, 1176–1900.* New York: Hill and Wang, 1999.

Kimiecik, Kathy. "The Strange Case of the Silver Lake Sea Serpent." *New York Folklore Society Newsletter* 9, no. 1 (Summer 1988): 10–11.

Lepper, Bradley T. and Jeff Gill. "The Newark Holy Stones." *Timeline* 17, no. 3 (May/June 2000): 17–25.

Loewenberg, Bert James. "Darwinism Comes to America, 1859–1900." *Mississippi Valley Historical Review* 28, no. 3 (December 1941): 339–368.

Millar, R. *The Piltdown Men.* New York: Ballantine Books, 1972.

Shermer, Michael. *Why People Believe Weird Things.* New York: W. H. Freeman, 1997.

Thompson, C. J. S. *The Mystery and Lore of Monsters: With Accounts of Some Giants, Dwarfs and Prodigies.* London: Williams & Norgate, 1930.

Time-Life Books. *Library of Curious and Unusual Facts: Hoaxes and Deceptions.* Alexandria, VA: Time-Life Books, 1991.

Twain, Mark. *Sketches New and Old.* New York: Harper & Brothers Publishers, 1922.

Walsh, John Evangelist. *Unraveling Piltdown: The Science Fraud of the Century and Its Solution.* New York: Random House, 1996.

Wiley, Gordon R., and Jeremy A. Sabloff. *A History of American Archaeology.* New York: W. H. Freeman, 1993.

Williams, Stephen. *Fantastic Archaeology: The Wild Side of North American Prehistory.* Philadelphia: University of Pennsylvania Press, 1991.

Photo Credits

INDEX

Note: Page numbers in **bold** refer to illustrations.